Kill the Editor

Millennial Mind Publishing
An imprint of American Book Publishing
American Book Publishing
P.O. Box 65624
Salt Lake City, UT 84165
www.american-book.com
Printed in the United States of America on acid-free paper.

Kill the Editor

Designed by George Shewchuk, design@american-book.com

Publisher's Note: **This publication is designed to provide accurate and authoritative information in regard to the subject matter covered. It is sold or distributed with the understanding that the publisher and author is not engaged in rendering legal, accounting, or other professional service. If legal advice or other expert assistance is required, the services of a competent professional person in a consultation capacity should be sought.**

ISBN 1-58982-182-3

Irby, John R., Kill the Editor

Special Sales

These books are available at special discounts for bulk purchases. Special editions, including personalized covers, excerpts of existing books, and corporate imprints, can be created in large quantities for special needs. For more information e-mail orders@american-book.com, 801-486-8639.

Kill the Editor

The often bizarre relationship with readers

By

John R. Irby

Dedication

There have been several great philosophers throughout time. Confucius comes to mind, as do, Plato and Socrates.

Confucius said: "By nature, men are nearly alike; by practice, they get to be wide apart." Plato said: "Wise men talk because they have something to say; fools, because they have to say something." Socrates said: "By all means marry; if you get a good wife, you'll be happy. If you get a bad one, you'll become a philosopher."

My father, circa 1990, said: "There comes a time in every man's life when he has to have a truck."

This book is dedicated to my father, Robert Durance Irby, a philosopher of sorts who has lived a happy life with a good wife.

While he didn't get a truck until he was just over seventy years old, my time has come much sooner. I have to have a truck. It doesn't matter that I don't absolutely need one. Unfortunately, I can't afford a new truck unless, of course, this book brings in some money.

Now at the age of eighty-three, my father has had plenty of philosophical material, beating colon cancer, surviving a triple bypass, and taking care of his wife—and my mother—who spends her days in and out of an Alzheimer's trance.

I began thinking philosophically as a six-year-old when I thought long and hard about the spanking my father gave me after peeing in my sister's wading pool.

As a senior in high school I wanted a car. I asked him. "Sure," he said, "if that's how you want to spend the money you've made [as a stock boy and sales clerk]."

It took me a few years, but I finally realized my dad taught me responsibility. I'm trying to model him in raising my children.

I've tried to teach Derren, eighteen, my oldest, responsibility, and he's been responsible for some of my madness.

His room is always a mess. He makes decisions for the wrong reasons. He has hair that I swear is half-way down his back. He mumbles when he talks, and shuffles when he walks. If he had worked a little harder, he could have gotten better grades.

I've learned a lot from my dad and others, and philosophy is nothing more than a pursuit of intellectual wisdom; a critical analysis of things.

I'm now able to do that with Derren. He graduated from high school in June 2003 and was one of two class speakers. He was the star in several school plays, wrote and directed a play for his senior project, and was assistant director in a musical. He was senior-class president. He worked part-time at a department store. He has stayed active in his church. He will attend college and work toward an education degree—to teach others.

Upon reflection, he's not all that different than I was when I was eighteen. Nor probably was I that different from my dad when we were the same age.

My dad, through his actions, taught me one of the greatest philosophies of life: "It is better to give than to receive."

He also demonstrated a work ethic. As much fun as I've had writing this book—telling life stories—it was also hard work. It wouldn't have been possible without my father. I love you dad.

Foreword

Newspaper journalism is a wild, often wonderful, often frustrating, often amazing career. And leading journalists is all that to the tenth power. Newspaper journalism also brings you into contact with society in all its good and bad, from the stunningly reasonable to the sadly insane. Ask any newspaper editor regarding some of the bizarre things they have witnessed, about the moments that are so funny you almost fall down laughing, and about the moments so sad you carry them around for weeks. You can be sure the resulting conversation will be a riveting experience.

One thing is certain: Editing a newspaper gives you a unique position to interact with a community, with the people who live there, with the people who work there, and to see it in an unadulterated light. That light isn't always flattering, but it is almost always interesting. As the cliché goes: Just when you think you've seen everything…

John Irby saw just about everything in uncountable ways in his twenty-five very accomplished years working in newsrooms across the country. He has worked at newspapers big and small, in communities liberal and conservative, in places sophisticated and simple. Through it all, as reporter, editor, and publisher, he has modeled all that is right about newspaper journalism: compassion for people and community, commitment to truth-telling and accuracy, following the highest road of ethical decision-making and decency. (That he now shares those values and his experiences with future journalists—as a much-acclaimed professor at the Murrow School of Communication at Washington State University—is a real bonus to the next generation.)

Through all the twists and turns of his career, John has never lost his sense of humor. And he had the good sense to save many of the interactions that tickled his funny bone or stood as profoundly sad commentary on the human condition.

Kill the Editor is a reflection of that. Some of what you read will amuse you, some will depress you. But it accurately represents a big part of the wild, wonderful world of editing a newspaper.

Peter Bhatia,
Executive editor of The Oregonian newspaper in Portland and 2003-04 president of the American Society of Newspaper Editors.

Prelude

Dear John,

I feel like I am writing a Dear John letter. Wait, I am! My name is Laura McAndrew. I was advised by you last year at Washington State University within the advertising degree program. I hope that is enough to base an identification of me because I can't think of another way for you to recall me.

As a student I remember your fondness for newspapers, which I did not understand until now.

I am writing to share with you how I enjoy newspapers also. I discovered this desire around the beginning of September when I moved back to Seattle to live with my two roommates who subscribe to *The Seattle Times*.

I love the paper almost to its entirety. My favorite sections are: Local News, Living, Religion (Saturday edition only), Crossword (America's favorite past time) and the Front Page. There is something about this medium that is very nostalgic. I like it when I unfold the paper and the smell of the freshly printed ink on paper wakes me up. To me the paper has become a simple pleasure of life.

Anyway, I just thought I would share this with you. I guess when you really enjoy something you can't help but share it with others.

If you get a chance, check out Dr. Dale Turner, religion columnist. His insight on life is captivating; you might like his work too!

Get your paper,

Laura M. McAndrew

Preface

In recent years, reporting the truth has become a job hazard for the world's media. In fact, it became a death sentence for more than one thousand journalists and media members who have been killed in the past ten years, through 2002, according to the International Federation of Journalists (IFJ).

The IFJ called 2002 a "year of targeting" as reporters on three continents died in assassinations for going after stories about terrorism, corruption, and criminal activity.

"These journalists paid the ultimate price for their stories," said IFJ General Secretary Aidan White in a press release announcing sixty-seven deaths in 2002. "It is time for the international community and the media industry to hunt down those who target journalists for asking the tough questions that help keep democracy intact."

Clearly the most grievous and sickening case was that of *Wall Street Journal* reporter Daniel Pearl who was kidnapped and videotaped while being slaughtered by his captors.

White said in the release: "This unprecedented and chilling display of brutality reminds journalists that global media are in the frontline of the struggle for democracy and human rights."

How many of those sixty-seven deaths were directly related to news-gathering, and how many came simply "in the line of duty" is debatable.

The Committee to Protect Journalists (CPJ), however, claimed in a January 2, 2003, news release that nineteen journalists were killed in 2002, a decline from thirty-seven in 2001, including eight while covering the war in Afghanistan.

New York-based CPJ said the nineteen murdered in 2002 was the fewest number killed in the line of duty since it began keeping records in 1985.

"While we are encouraged to see the number of deaths decrease this year, journalists are still being targeted and assassinated for doing their jobs," said CPJ Executive Director Ann K. Cooper.

"Drug traffickers in Brazil, paramilitary groups in Colombia, and corrupt politicians in the Philippines are trying to silence journalists through intimidation and murder, and it has to stop."

Another group, Reporters Without Borders, said in January 2003 that twenty-five journalists were killed in 2002.

In at least ten other cases, the group was reported as saying in *Editor & Publisher* magazine, "the state, especially the army, was directly involved...In many countries, authorities used the global fight against terrorism as an excuse to arrest reporters, including journalists accused of supporting rebels in Chechnya or Colombia."

Reporters Without Borders also reported that at least 692 journalists were arrested in 2002.

And as late as October 15, 2003, the World Association of Newspapers said fifty-one journalists had been killed on the job because of their work in 2003, an increase over forty-six in 2002, driven by the war in Iraq and other conflicts.

The deaths, attacks, arrests, and international atrocities have been well documented for years.

The World Association of Newspapers (WAN), a Paris-based group, said twenty-four journalists were killed for doing their jobs, not just while at work, but in the line of duty, in 2000. CPJ reported sixteen were murdered for covering the story—no matter what the journalists reported, positive or negative.

"Most were killed in countries where assassins have learned they can kill journalists with impunity," the CPJ report concluded.

Attacks on the Press in 2000, an annual survey by CPJ, said many were assassinated for their work in countries from Bangladesh to Uruguay, with Colombia, Russia, and Sierra Leone being the sites of the deadliest assignments (three were killed in each nation).

"Killers were brought to justice in very, very few of these cases, and we think that's why year after year there are a handful of countries that keep turning up on this list," Cooper said.

China jailed the most journalists in 2000 (twenty-two), and there were 600 cases of media repression in 131 countries, according to CPJ. Those included assassination, assault, imprisonment, censorship, and harassment.

Many journalists have been targeted for assassination in attempts to stop their reporting. Intentional killing, in fact, is the leading cause of job-related death for journalists.

Aside from worldwide deaths, newspapers have also seen the greatest drain in journalists in twenty-five years, according to the American Society of Newspaper Editors (ASNE), which revealed in early 2002 that nearly two thousand editorial employees left the industry in the past year.

Announced at ASNE's annual convention, it was reported that the nearly two thousand employees left medium-sized newspapers—primarily from layoffs, buyouts, and early retirements—all in the name of cost reductions.

The last several years have also seen incredible ethical lapses and credibility concerns, the most recent being the Jayson Blair fiasco at the *New York Times*.

That high-profile case, however, is only one of several lapses in judgment of reporters and editors nationwide, ranging from a newspaper in Washington state publishing a false story to aid government officials, to reporters in Salt Lake City selling information on the Elizabeth Smart case to the *National Enquirer*, to Iraqi War media representatives trying to smuggle back artifacts for personal pleasure and gain.

Kill the Editor, however, isn't a book about journalists who are being murdered, attacked, or leaving the business for any variety of reasons, including ethical terminations.

It is a book dedicated to journalists who have lost their lives because of their calling, or have left their calling because of mismanagement or some other form of professional abuse.

While most reporters and editors are not subjected to kidnap, torture, or murder, many are routinely exposed to verbal threats and attacks, sometimes even physical violence.

Kill the Editor is a book about many things. It is a compilation of abuses by, and random thoughts of, newspaper readers. It is a book about an industry that needs immediate and significant change. It's a book about racism in society. And it's a book about overly opinionated fanatics who are closed to compromise.

It's also a book about severely troubled individuals, with differing degrees of personal and mental problems. It's a book about people who lack pity and compassion toward one another. It's a book about Americans and their relationship with newspapers.

But most of all, it's a book about people, too many of whom act in strange or idiotic ways.

Contents

Chapter One

Sad but True

It's easy to appreciate the overall wit, wisdom, and humor of legendary writer, editor, and social critic Henry Louis Mencken. It's also fashionable—and appropriate—to condemn specific racist statements and beliefs associated with him.

Nevertheless, an argument could be made that many of Mencken's writings, from the early 1900s through the mid-century and before his death, still ring true in relationship to American newspapers. Here are two:

"The volume of mail that comes in to a…newspaper…is no index of anything, except that you happen to attract a lot of idiots, because most people who write letters to newspapers are fools. Intelligent people seldom do it—they do it sometimes—but not often."

1. "This (working at a newspaper) would be a great

business, if not for the reader."

Mencken was right. But since it took a nearly thirty-year newspaper career to figure it out, maybe I'm the idiot.

Mencken was also a vitriolic critic of his own industry:

"The average newspaper, especially of the better sort, has the intelligence of a hillbilly evangelist, the courage of a rat, the fairness of a prohibitionist boob-jumper, the information of a high-school janitor, the taste of a designer of celluloid valentines and the honor of a police-station lawyer."

Right again.

Newspapers will never be great businesses, not only because of foolish readers, but rather because of too much involvement from too many corporate owners who have an apparent inability to perceive and correct industry woes.

And in the process of decline, voices across America are being muted and homogenized by corporate giants who have traded, merged, and sold properties—all for bottom-line considerations. Today, the media is converging, which will further erode independent voices as companies are now allowed to own newspapers and TV stations in the same market.

The top twenty newspaper companies in America—in an effort to control, group, and cluster the print media—have garnered 62 percent of the nation's circulation, according to *Facts About Newspapers,* Newspaper Association of America (NAA), www.naa.org. And while the annual profit margin average is 30 percent or more for many, eleven high-profile groups that arguably hold higher journalistic standards, still average 22 percent, according to *American Journalism Review,* December 2000. Gaudy, some claim, in comparison to many industries. Grocery stores, as a comparison, are ecstatic with a 5 percent annual profit margin.

Newspapers are simply very profitable.

Clearly post-September 11 profits declined, in direct proportion to the economic downturn, but as the newspaper industry has done for years it has corrected the downward spiral with space cutbacks, human buyouts, and layoffs.

The industry is once again turning the profit corner.

While clustering takes on different forms, depending upon group ownership strategy, it has been defined by Dirks, Van Essen & Murray, the most active merger-and-acquisition firm in the newspaper industry, as "dailies in adjacent counties."

In just over ten years, there has been a 16 percent increase in clustering, from 19 percent of all daily newspapers in the United States in 1990 to 35 percent of the 1,457 dailies today.

Are newspaper groups foolish? Not, so far, in business matters. But that time may soon come as the industry suffers a tremendous credibility gap with readers, and maybe most importantly, faces an onslaught of competition from other and new media.

As an example, the Internet is already starting to replace newspapers for the eighteen-to-twenty-four-year-old group, according to a poll taken by a Chicago-based consortium of business school technology professors. The Round Table Group **reported in a survey that 67**

percent of the age group used the Net to gather information. Of that number, 57 percent said they get better information from the Net than from newspapers.

The poll also showed the traditional strong newspaper markets—those with higher incomes and education—also leaving newspapers for electronic options.

Media regular-usage trends also show major declines not only in newspapers but also local, world, and national TV and radio news. Internet usage for news, however, is increasing.

An NAA Market & Business Analysis Department "Fast Fact" in Presstime **magazine revealed the following about regular media usage between the years 1997 and 2000:**

Daily newspaper has declined from 51 to 46 percent; local TV news dropped from 63 percent to 55 percent; world-national TV news fell from 42 to 37 percent; radio news dropped from 49 to 43 percent; Internet news has increased from 7 to 18 percent.

Newspaper readers are primarily white—and aging. Many in the industry claimed this problem would be resolved by nonreading teens who would grow into adulthood, complete with a newspaper reading habit. It was a myth that young people, as they settled into communities and aged, would read newspapers. And it isn't likely to happen in the future, in part because newspapers continue to pander to primarily aging white male readers at the expense of others including minorities, women, and the young.

Attracting a new generation of readers may be the best

chance of salvation for the industry. The hope for tomorrow's newspapers is likely Generation Y, those born between 1977 and 1995.

"The next generation of Americans is wired, worldly, and wondering if the news their parents read isn't a bit like an Oldsmobile, a vehicle for an earlier generation," said Chris Peck, editor of the Memphis Commercial Appeal. "Their music is different, their cultural icons are different, their values are different from the Generation X and Baby Boomers before them."

That, however, is a whole different story.

This book is primarily about newspaper readers, some of whom are foolish, at least in their actions. But as any fool knows, not all newspaper readers are idiots or crazy. It may even be just a small percentage, but the number is certainly higher than most would expect.

Readership surveys conducted by paid marketing companies, or organizations supportive of the industry, won't even address the issue. They don't want to know or identify an "idiot factor."

They will, however, show a positive newspaper readership demographic, despite many negatives such as year-over-year declining circulation and audience (specifically minorities, women, and teens), and place the best possible statistical spin on the numbers.

Advertisers are routinely told that newspaper readers, among other things, are highly educated and have healthy incomes. It's an attractive market for those who advertise goods and services. But offering those same goods and services through newspaper advertisement to "idiots" would simply be idiotic. So, researchers never identify the percentage of fools who read newspapers.

Editors, however, know who they are and what they have to say, but generally, like researchers, don't want to acknowledge, talk, or write about that segment of readers.

That doesn't change the fact every newspaper editor in America has received a significant number of phone calls, letters, or other contacts that aren't only idiotic, but often incoherent ramblings, personal verbal attacks, and/or physical threats.

For years I gave speeches to Rotarians and other civic-minded groups of men (and later women), and quoted Mencken about how readers prevented newspapers from being a great business. I did that so I could take issue with his statement and proudly proclaim my professional loyalty by saying it was my philosophy that working in the newspaper industry was a great business because of readers. I reasoned that without readers there would be no newspapers.

That is a true statement.

But where I went wrong was reasoning that readers make newspapers a "great" business. Readers—foolish or wise—only ensure the business.

No one today is about to guarantee readership. Many an athlete has been able to use statistical information to make a case for viability, say for the Heisman Trophy or most valuable player awards. But statistical review has become a nightmare for newspapers. Consider the following from NAA:

The 2002 average adult weekday readership was 55.4 percent, down from 77.6 percent in 1970.

More than 300 daily newspapers have gone out of business in the past forty years—from 1,772 in 1950 to 1,457 in 2002.

Newspaper circulation in 2002 was 55.2 million, falling from a peak of almost 63 million in 1987. During that same period, the U.S. population grew to 272 million from 203 million, a 69 million increase (34 percent).

"A newspaper is a device for making the ignorant more ignorant and the crazy crazier," according to Mencken. More and more editors would probably agree as they are admitting that newspapers aren't as much fun as they used to be.

Many are leaving their jobs to become university professors, public relations practitioners, or to work in some other related field. They are making less money, but enjoying life more.

The profession—and the industry—was once well respected. Today, newspapers no longer command a high level of trust as an institution vital to society, one that is accurate in its dissemination of news and information. Editors are often thought of less favorably by the general public than used-car salesmen, who, rightly or wrongly, have always been considered suspect.

More Mencken: "No one in this world, so far as I know—and I have researched the records for years, and employed agents to help me—has ever lost money by underestimating the intelligence of the great masses of the plain people. Nor has anyone ever lost public office thereby." And, "...the average citizen is half-witted, and hence not to be trusted to either his own devices or his own thoughts."

Mencken also published letters to the editor that violently denounced himself, because he believed people liked to read about abuse. He was right.

In nearly thirty years in the newspaper industry, more than half as an editor and publisher, it became clear that readers sometimes wanted to "kill the editor."

More often than not, they didn't want to actually "kill" him or her, but some were so upset with their local newspaper editor they made threats, sometimes even physical. This book is a compilation of interesting, intriguing, bizarre, and sad stories—most of which have never been published. In some cases they have been slightly edited for clarity and canons of taste, but every effort was made to not alter the message or provide one where it was absent.

Remember O. J. Simpson? How could anyone forget?

During the trial, Julianne McKinney was listed on correspondence as director of the Association of National Security Alumni Electronic Surveillance Project in Silver Springs, Maryland.

Sounds like an impressive position. A think tank, maybe.

The following letters, reportedly from McKinney, were addressed to O. J. attorney Johnnie Cochran, and came from a reader with these handwritten comments: "Where is the press coverage on this subject? Is this area off limits? Why? Doesn't the public have a right to know what's going on? Yes, truth can be stranger than fiction."

In the letters, McKinney offered Cochran a Flip Wilson (comedian) sort-of defense: "The devil made me do it." Only in this case it was: "The government made me do it." (CIA, FBI, spooks?) She also offered trial advice and strategy.

The credo listed on the letters of the Association of National Security Alumni, by the way, was: "...Covert actions are counterproductive and damaging to the national interests of the United States. They are inimical to the operation of an effective national intelligence system and corruptive of civil liberties, including the functioning of the judiciary and a free press. Most importantly, they contradict the principles of democracy, national self-determination and international law to which the United States is publicly committed."

Clearly, Cochran and "The Dream Team" found better defenses—gloves that didn't fit, Mark Fuhrman, Kato Kalin, an arguably noneffective prosecution team, a questionable judge, and favorable jury.

Conspiracy theorists read on.

February 1, 1995
Johnnie Cochran, Esq
4929 Wilshire Boulevard
Suite 1010
Los Angeles, CA 99010

Dear Mr. Cochran:

The more I hear of the circumstances surrounding O. J. Simpson's case, the more I am inclined to suspect he has been the target of a U.S. Intelligence operation. Today's testimony concerning Mr. Simpson's "dreams" has heightened that concern.

I am a former U.S. Intelligence officer, trained at the national level. I am currently the Director of a Project which is focused on the widespread involuntary human experimentation which is now ongoing in this country, involving the use of directed-energy weapons, surveillance and "neurocybernetics" systems. (The Department of Defense refers to these latter as "psychotechnologies.") These operations, which are exceptionally brutal, qualify as attempts at "mind control."

A classic "mind control" operation involves, among other things, the following: (1) Long-term, round-the-clock physical and electronic surveillances for purposes of collecting "personalia" on, and biological specimens from, a targeted individual for future exploitation; (2) overt and covert forms of repetitive harassment for purposes of studying the experimentee's capacity to handle extreme stress; (3) directed-energy harassment for purposes of inducing extreme disorientation and debilitating forms of pain (involving technologies which are currently characterized as "less-than-lethal" weapons and surveillance systems by the U.S. Department of Justice); (4) experimentation with neurocybernetics and psychotechnologies, which have a capacity to induce quasi-subliminal "voices in the head" and which, when the experimentee is asleep can influence the evolutionary development of dreams; (5) long-term manipulation of the experimentee, to compel behavior and statements which, in the long-term, will be self-discrediting; (6) isolation and financial impoverishment of the experimentee; and (7) continual terrorization of the experimentee for purposes compelling an act of violence, whether suicide or murder.

When disclosing to Shipps (Ron, a former friend of O. J. and Nicole Simpson) that he had dreamed about Nicole's murder, Mr. Simpson clearly would have had no way of knowing dreams can be induced by this government's array of psychotechnologies. His disclosures to Shipp— characteristic of a long-term "mind-control" operation—are now being used as evidence of mental imbalance. I sincerely hope Mr. Simpson did not also confide to his "friends" that he has also heard "voices in his head," since that, too, will be used as evidence of mental imbalance. (As a matter of interest, and should the subject be pushed in court, this quasi-subliminal auditory input can be obstructed by physical means. The U.S. Government's so-called psychotechnologies are not infallible.)

The LAPD (Los Angeles Police Department), incidentally, is well aware of these technologies. Their Special Intelligence Section (SIS), in fact, may be participating in some of the operations referenced above. You will note, in the enclosed bulletin published by the National Institute of Justice, that the NIJ is working very closely with law enforcement agencies and corrections facilities in accumulating data on the effectiveness of these various directed-energy systems. What is not reported in this bulletin is that the testing of these technologies is being covertly conducted, under wholly involuntary circumstances. The experimentation now ongoing in U.S. prison and jail systems is quite vicious.

I am aware that Mr. Simpson's trial may not be the proper venue for exposing this type of experimentation, even as it may pertain to his case specifically. My reason for writing is to alert you to the fact that Mr. Simpson could very well have been targeted as far back as 1989 for experimentation, and that the murder of his wife and Goldman (Ron) could very well have been intended to be the culminating point of his particular experiment.

It was probably wrongfully assumed by the agencies engaged in Mr. Simpson's long-term surveillance that he would commit suicide immediately following the news of his wife's death. Suicide is the ultimate form of self-discrediting and closure. Fortunately that did not happen. The haphazard gaps and flaws in the Prosecution's case strongly suggest Mr. Simpson's suicide was and, perhaps, still is expected. Put another way, the Prosecution clearly had not banked on Mr. Simpson's survival.

The purpose of this letter is to shed some further light on Mr. Simpson's current circumstances. The murders were not entirely senseless insofar as these experiments are concerned. They are now being used to cynically demonstrate the ease with which public opinion can be molded and manipulated by a controlled media. A public—groomed to think stereotypically that a spousal abuser will invariably kill—will not accept the fact murders can be committed by persons who witnessed sporadic acts of spousal abuse during the course of a long-term surveillance.

Mr. Simpson may have been nothing more than a U.S. Intelligence guinea pig; however, he is still a living guinea pig and, for that reason alone, he is very fortunate. Most of these experimentees, when pushed to an act of violence, do not survive.

I do not believe Mr. Simpson is guilty and accordingly wish you the best of luck with your defense, regardless of what approach you take.

A second letter was reportedly sent on April 17, 1995.

Dear Mr. Cochran:

When writing to you last February, I alerted you to the fact that Mr. Simpson may be the target of a U.S. Intelligence-based operation which, at least preliminarily, might have been intended to affect his suicide. A copy of my letter is attached. In that letter, I pointed out that this government, and cooperative police agencies, have technologies at their disposal which have the capacity, as a minimum, to induce "voices in the head" (and the associated ability to induce dreams).

Certain additional allegations surfaced during the course of Mr. Simpson's ongoing trial that once again point to the possibility of a classic government operation. While, again, I recognize the courtroom is perhaps not the proper venue for introducing these matters on Mr. Simpson's behalf, I do nevertheless regard it as essential that you be furnished this information for your disposition as you see fit.

Standard procedure in these involuntary human experiments is to target an experimentee's joints, cartilage and spinal nerves with highly focused directed-energy (such as radar) for purposes of producing crippling arthritic or bursitis-like symptoms. The targeting can be blocked. The pain ceases abruptly when the targeting is terminated; and such inflammation as might have been produced disappears within a very short period of time without a need for medical treatment.

Mr. Simpson's capacity to produce a physical-fitness video after being diagnosed as arthritic suggests to me his symptoms may have been deliberately induced by directed-energy means during a lengthy period preceding the making of that film; and the targeting ceased during the period when he produced the film. His having made the film, of course, had the effect of discrediting his claims regarding the arthritis. Under the circumstances, you might want to take a closer look at the person(s) who had encouraged him to make the film, and at the methods of persuasion employed. You might also want to take a closer look at the person(s) who knew this otherwise-obscure film existed, and who made it a point of ensuring it was rapidly introduced into evidence.

Another standard procedure in these "mind-control" operations involves the inflicting of laser cuts on experimentees. The cuts, at least in the case of most experimentees, are generally a quarter to a half-inch in length, based on obviously short-burst transmissions. They also resemble and feel like bleeding paper cuts. They are inflicted generally when the experimentee's hand is raised; i.e., exclusive of any presence of paper. The same technologies have been employed on certain military installations (such as on the territories surrounding NORAD) in so-called "UFO" cattle-mutilation scenarios. The same technologies are also now being touted by the medical establishment as being wondrous new surgical tools.

If Mr. Simpson was not in fact handling paper when he first felt the "sting" of the cut on his finger, and if he was standing near a window or skylight (or outdoors) when he sustained that cut, you might want to take a closer look at this wondrous new surgical tool as it might pertain to that conveniently-timely cut on his finger.

Another standard procedure in these mind-control operations is the thermal heating of experimentees by means of microwaves and/or by what we think might be infrared laser energy. Thermal heating is generally employed to induce stress in an experimentee, or to aggravate a pre-existing condition of stress, if only to study the experimentee's capacity to function under these circumstances.

Mr. Simpson experienced what may have been microwave-induced thermal heating while riding in that limousine to the airport. His claims, during his trip, of having felt extraordinarily hot in 70-degree weather are being used, of course, to portray a man riddled with fear and guilt. Fortunately he did not hysterically demand that the driver stop the car so he could get out and cool off, and that he did not behave otherwise in noticeably bizarre fashion. Microwave heating can produce extreme (and unexplainable) anger in certain susceptible experimentees.

The fact that Mr. Simpson's limousine driver did not experience the same symptoms points to a possibility steps were taken to ensure this type of targeting would be highly focused. This would require either a tracking device (transponder) be implanted in the back seat of the limousine or that Mr. Simpson, himself, be injected with a transponder for tracking purposes. I am enclosing some literature concerning injectible [sic] transponders. Microwave and cellular-phone towers are being used in a large number of these types of experiments and may have played a role on the route traversed by Mr. Simpson and his chauffer on the night in question.

Finally, and this is a matter which I discussed with Mr. Douglas (Carl, member of The Dream Team) in late 1994, I urge you to take a closer look at what is happening to the jury. I am aware Mr. Douglas did not take me seriously when I alerted him to the fact that various jury members— if sequestration became inevitable—might become "ill" as the result of directed-energy targeting. That three jurors recently became ill on the same day has prompted my resurfacing this matter.

Direct-energy technologies have the capacity to produce a wide variety of symptoms that resemble illness produced by microbes and viruses. The symptoms disappear when the targeting terminates or is blocked. The symptoms are also notable as phenomena in the medical field, which elude being linked to known etiologies (assignment of a cause, an origin, or a reason for something).

Infrasound, for example, can produce massive headaches, abdominal pains, nausea, vomiting and diarrhea. The symptoms can be halted abruptly. Extremely low frequency electromagnetic energy can produce intense lethargy, unwarranted fatigue and disorientation, such as are now popularly attributed to "chronic fatigue syndrome." These symptoms, too, can be abruptly terminated. Radar targeting of the reproductive organs can cause all sorts of disruption. This, too, can be obstructed. And high energy fields (scalar waves) built up in sealed environments can produce burning eyes, raw throats, running noses and other symptoms resembling a flu. These symptoms disappear as soon as a window is opened. I hope your jurors are not sequestered in a permanently sealed environment.

Also, if this is a government operation, you can be certain your jurors will have been deliberately impaneled for purposes of fostering dissention so as to bring about a mistrial. The juror who engaged in the physical battery of other jurors and who is otherwise deporting herself in inflammatory fashion, needs to be removed immediately—a matter you have no doubt already considered.

You may also be certain—again, if this is a government operation—that all of your jury members are under close electronic surveillance. As a minimum, the area of sequestration needs to be subjected to ongoing, round-the-clock technical monitoring, to ensure that neither directed-energy systems nor other more traditional forms of surveillance technologies are being used. You also need to know who the jurors' surrounding tenants might happen to be. Surrounding rooms (to include upstairs and downstairs) and rooms in adjacent buildings are routinely used as bases of operation in these government exercises.

Your spectrum analyzer (should you acquire one) should have the capacity, as a minimum, to monitor acoustical frequencies and electromagnetic frequencies in the 28 Megahertz range which latter frequencies are reserved (for unexplained purposes) exclusive for government use. If you do decide to take this precaution, your technicians should be accompanied at all times by defense team personnel.

Finally, and this is the reason why I had called Mr. Douglas in the first place, the ailments which Mr. Simpson experienced in his jail cell resembled those which can be produced by directed energy. I strongly recommend Mr. Simpson be equipped with a portable EMF detector with a limited direction-finding capability (loop antenna), just to rule out the prospect of a recurrence of his ailments under non-biological circumstances.

I do have one additional minor tip regarding your team's recent attempts at establishing a conspiratorial relationship between Fung (Dennis, crime lab specialist) and Fuhrman (Mark, police department detective). If this is a government operation, you can be certain steps have been taken to ensure all participants in the conspiracy have a cover of plausible deniability.

These government operations appear to be based on an

infrastructure resembling the cellular organization of well-known revolutionary groups. What you need to look at are Fung's and Fuhrman's potential links to the LAPD's Special Intelligence Section. Both, if willing participants in a conspiracy, will have taken their orders from a common source. The SIS, which has an established history of civil and human rights abuses under conspiratorial circumstances, may be that common link.

In closing, I would like to note that your Mr. Barry Scheck (Dream Team member) has been doing a phenomenal job in exposing the flaws in the LAPD's collection of evidence. Keep up the good work. In the meantime, I hope the foregoing will be some limited assistance.

Limited assistance? Who was she kidding? Heck, O. J. would have been declared innocent in record time—by reason of insanity—if Cochran had run McKinney's defense up the flag pole from Day One, and followed her trial advice and strategy.

While the above two letters are longer than most received by editors, they are, in many ways, typical of many newspaper readers and letter writers.

Let them serve as an introduction to what lies ahead. But first, in chapter 2, a look at some of my favorite stories and journalists—many of whom are a bit crazy in their own ways.

Chapter Two

Welcome to My Asylum

Sex has long been an interest at newspapers, as it is just about anywhere. Surveys have consistently shown the public will read about it—as long as they are not a part of what is being reported.

There are a million stories.

One of the best is about a city editor and reporter one hot afternoon on deadline.

She was a decent reporter. Not the best, by anyone's standards, but nor was she the worst.

She certainly had assets.

As a reporter, she didn't often make factual mistakes. But as a writer, she was pedestrian, at best. Unfortunately, she was also a slow writer.

She was of average intelligence. Smart enough generally to ask the right questions, but a bit flighty, absentminded, and naïve.

Much of what she said could be taken more than one way. But then that was part of her charm.

The men in the newsroom also acknowledged, on a regular basis, their interest in her. She had simple facial beauty and, what was termed in that era, a "major league body."

There was only one problem. As a recent young divorcee with two small children, she made it clear she was available for serious dating; but along with that came the fear of husband entrapment.

The metro editor was separated and heading toward a divorce of his own. Jane made her move. He was interested, and horny. Before he knew it, she had the two getting together for a Saturday afternoon date in the park with her kids. She told everyone in the newsroom.

Yikes!

Friday afternoon on deadline, the day before the date, she was working on a page-one story. All of the other reporters had turned in their copy, which had been edited. It was time for the final call for her copy.

The metro editor made sure all reporters made their deadlines. He made the trains run on time. He was the maestro.

"Hey," he yelled across the room, in front of about fifty other reporters and editors. "I need it [your copy] now. I can't wait any longer for it [the story]. I've got to have it."

She looked up and yelled back across the room: "I'm coming, I'm coming…I'm just slow."

The metro editor was speechless. The reporting staff was

hysterical with laughter. The beautiful reporter was clueless. The date never took place.

NAZIS ON PARADE:

Even though he was often disparaged by critics, Norman Rockwell, and his art, is widely loved by average, and not so average, Americans.

The same can't be said for George Lincoln Rockwell, "spiritual" leader and founder of the American Nazi Party.

The young reporter was asked by the city editor to interview the group, which had phoned in because they "had a story to tell."

As any reporter knows, research is king. Without proper background information, interviews can take strange twists.

He went to the newspaper morgue and found out "Commander" Rockwell and the American Nazi Party were "dedicated to the preservation of the White Race, the Aryan Republic, and Western-European cultural heritage."

He also learned this might be a difficult assignment. He was the son of a minister, who had taught him the love of Christ. He had lived during his formative years in Compton, California, near Watts. The inner city of Los Angeles. He had attended Pepperdine University in the heart of Southwest LA.

He had always lived a multicultural life. While no one is completely colorblind, he was close.

And now he had to put his feelings aside and interview hate mongers. These people never considered politically correct terms of the era such as African-American or black. They used the N-word—and still do.

How could he interview this group?

He was nervous, and for good reason.

After getting lost in the neighborhood, he finally found the San Gabriel Valley home in a residential/light commercial-zoned area that served as the party headquarters.

It was a creepy house. All the windows were covered from the inside. Paint was peeling and falling by the minute. It was a cold, gray day.

He climbed up the three steps at the entry area and knocked on the door.

Dogs barked. Lots of dogs.

While it seemed like an eternity, the door finally opened, probably about fifteen seconds after he knocked.

He first noticed the dogs. Four Doberman pinschers, with aggressive and belligerent attitudes, continued to bark and snarl.

A command was then given by one of the four men at the door, and the dogs stared with angry eyes at the reporter.

While backgrounding for the interview assignment, the reporter had learned about Herr (Louis) Dobermann. He lived in the southern part of Germany in the early to late 1800s. He was a tax collector, night watchman, dog catcher, and supervisor for a slaughter house.

He determined he needed a dog to accompany him on his rounds, especially for protection when he carried tax collection money.

If the dogs at the door weren't scary enough, the four men were not poster boys for their so-called purity of blood or race. They were scrounges. They smelled. They had unshaven faces and shoulder-length, greasy hair. Those were their good qualities.

Each one had a pistol strapped on his waist, and two had some sort of shotgun or rifle in their arms.

They clearly dressed in an effort to impress. But they were not impressive, only a bit scary and pathetic.

They invited the reporter in.

As it turned out, the interview went as well as could be expected.

The American Nazi party members had a story to tell, so they weren't about to kill the messenger.

But the content was weak. They preached over and over again the same sad, racist story.

The story, while well-written, ran deep inside the second section of the paper.

RING...RING:

A newspaper reporter was assigned to write an obituary about a prominent citizen. A head shot (called mug shot) was needed. A copy clerk went to the photo morgue and pulled a shot of the well-known gentleman talking on a telephone. The editor, who approved the obituary and wrote the headline, did not see the photo. The headline: Death calls

CAN YOU SAY LIBEL?

A copy editor couldn't think of a pithy saying to place under the head shot of the state's new bar association president. So, he decided, he'd put a "dummy" tag line under the name and come back after editing the story, to write the tag line when his creative juices would, once again, be flowing.

There was only one problem. He forgot and the dummy tag line was published under the name of the new president of the state's top organization of attorneys. What did it say?…*another crazy mother*

THANKSGIVING DAY:

Two editors were banging out the sports rewrites and editing wire copy late one night. A girls' softball coach called to report the score of his game. The editor in charge of the desk that night wrote the story.

He committed the cardinal sin of journalism. He thought he'd be a bit clever and have a little fun, because he knew the other editor working with him would read the story before publication and catch his tomfoolery.

But the second editor got busy, and he knew his partner on the desk was a solid journalist—which he was—so he sent the story to print without an edit. Here's what was published: "What's a turkey like this doing coaching such a good team?"

P.S. The offending editors went on to become sports editors of two of the largest newspapers in America.

LET IT SNOW:

Headlines are often included at the top of stand-alone photos, with the caption under the picture. One photo showed mounds and mounds of snow. But the headline, shocking and pithy, was something special:

S--- Load of Snow

THANKS FOR NOTHING:

The feature section of this newspaper carried the following dateline information on its cover—"Day Month Year."

You guessed it. One day the information was not filled in and the cover ran with no precise day or month or even year—only "Day Month Year."

HELLO, SWEETHEART:

In the good old days, veteran reporters often called in from the field on deadline with information that someone on the rewrite desk would fashion into a story. While it hadn't happened for years, one reporter tried to resurrect days gone by.

The phone rang. The young female reporter, her first day on the job at this metro, answered and heard: "Hello, sweetheart, give me rewrite."

She didn't know what to do so she started taking dictation. But suddenly she spied him across the room, where he was jabbering on the phone, too drunk to write.

DEAF AND DUMB:

A reporter at a suburban newspaper called an editor to say he was too sick to come to work. The reporter, however, was sitting directly behind the editor, who was nearly deaf—and fairly stupid.

The editor told the executive editor, who was standing at his desk, that the star reporter wouldn't be coming to work.

The executive editor then banged his hand on the desk and gestured behind the nearly deaf editor to indicate the smiling reporter, who had just called in sick, from an office phone.

OOPS!

A sports story was explaining how a quarterback got "sacked," ending all hope for a comeback in this particular game. Not exactly a man-bites-dog kind of story, but it became an offbeat one when the typesetter typed a "u" instead of an "a."

CATHOLIC GIRLS:

High school sports reporters are made for the beat. They are energetic. For some strange reason, they would rather cover little Tommy Smith fumbling the ball on a likely touchdown run for the state high school championship, than National Football League MVPs.

This reporter was doing his best to impress the other sports writers, who had all cautioned him he might be writing just a bit too colorfully.

Nonetheless he turned in two stories one day. The first was about a high school football running back. The second was about a high school girl's basketball team.

In the football story he wrote: "He's harder to tackle than a Coke machine."

The desk editor called him over and dryly asked: "Hey kid, you ever tried to tackle a Coke machine?"

"No," he said.

"Then how do you know how hard it is?"

"I guess I don't."

"Then you have two options. Number one, you can change the copy to something readers will understand. Or, you can go out and try to tackle a Coke machine and come back and add even more detail to how hard it is to tackle a Coke machine. But I bet you in advance $100 that your running back is easier to tackle than a Coke machine."

The reporter went from one extreme to another. His revised copy simply said the running back was difficult to tackle.

His phraseology in the second story about the girl's basketball team was much more offensive, but just as stupid.

In talking about how a team was doing lots of scoring, he couldn't resist this sexual pun. "You know how those Catholic girls are."

The slot man called him over again. "Hey, do you really think this is wise, to say 'You know how those Catholic girls are'?"

"Well, he said, I'm Catholic, so I do have some knowledge about it."

"Take it out. Rewrite it."

"Well, OK."

GETTING EVEN:
A newspaper intern was assigned to edit and write a headline for a story about a university president signing his new book at a bookstore later in the week. The president of the Catholic University was also a priest.

The intern had attended the same school and wasn't happy the priest/university president had stopped a visiting lecture by Planned Parenthood.

She said she was only "fooling around" when she wrote the headline, which was published:

"Nazi priest promotes his book"

Even though the priest was a forgiving sort, newspaper management didn't think it was funny. The young woman was fired.

HOLY MOTHER, FULL OF GRACE:

A reporter was covering an Easter play/pageant and wrote the following: "The sobs of Mary Magdalene could be heard up and down the streets as she watched her son Jesus…"

Only one problem—if the reporter had checked her biblical facts she would have learned that Mary Magdalene was not Jesus' mother.

Chapter Three

A Different Kind of Business

It didn't take long as a journalist to understand that working for a newspaper wasn't exactly the same as a factory assignment, soda jerking, or department store servicing.

For instance, there isn't a great deal of danger involved in placing two-sizes-too-small pumps on a woman's feet in the J. C. Penney shoe department. Unless of course she takes offense to the subtle suggestions that the glass slipper doesn't fit.

And there aren't too many threats making freeway fence posts at Southwest Steel Rolling Mills, the only steel mill in inner-city Los Angeles.

Nor was it too difficult to make change as a clerk at the 7-Eleven convenience store (even though it apparently is today for some teens).

Young workers find success in those types of jobs, and

others, throughout high school and college—and sometimes even right after graduation in difficult economic times.

However, the time had come to become a professional reporter, which would include such assignments as viewing dead bodies and being placed in jeopardy in a number of ways.

The clues to this unusual business were prevalent.

But young reporters fresh out of college aren't always allowed to come up with their own story ideas. It's for good reason, as twenty-one-year-old men and women have limited knowledge and experience, even though they know they are smarter than their parents (something they learned at about the age of thirteen).

It was the first day as a professional reporter. The grizzled, veteran city editor barked: "Hey, kid, call this woman on the phone."

Eyes wide as moons, he barked excitedly as he talked: "She's got a heck of a story to tell, kid. Something about how she escaped from a bunch of people who were out to get her. Get a good story and we'll lead the front page with it tomorrow."

A front-page story? Every new reporter dreams of it. When the opportunity is presented, staff writers get stoked. After dialing the number and listening to three rings, a woman answered. Following brief introductions she growled, "Call me Anna."

"So, Anna, what's this about getting away from people that were after you?"

"They broke into my home," she said in a high-pitched screech.

"Who's after you? How did you get away?"

"I didn't get away," Anna said, angered at the silly question. "They broke into my house when I wasn't there and I didn't know about it until I got home. How many times do I have to tell you?"

That was the first.

"Well, did you report it to the police?"

"Yes," Anna said, angrily screaming. "They took a report, but they haven't done anything. You know how the cops are. They're worthless. I've been telling you reporters about this for several months now!"

Notes couldn't be scribbled as fast as Anna could talk.

Then a roar of laughter came from the other reporters in the newsroom.

What was so funny?

A reporter passed a note that read: "Ask her what was taken."

"So, Anna, what did they take?"

There was a long silence. The question was repeated, "What did they take?"

An agitated Anna screamed, "Don't you know? I told you this a thousand times before. They took toilet paper…all my toilet paper. I haven't had any for years and I just don't know what I'm going to do."

The newsroom was in stitches.

How does a new reporter handle a practical joke? How does a new reporter deal with a source that obviously isn't, as the cliché goes, "dealing with a full deck"?

Anna rambled for another five minutes. She was harmless, but obviously mentally unbalanced. The conversation didn't end until a promise was made to call this lonely woman back from time to time, to listen, and be her new best friend.

As it turned out, Anna was a newsroom regular, who even stopped by the office from time to time to provide reporters with cookies and the latest scoops.

A long-time city resident, Anna did have some connections and again, as the cliché goes, she knew where "all the bodies were buried."

While most of her tips focused on toilet-paper capers and other delusions, from time to time she provided information that lead to uncovering city hall misdeeds and mishaps.

Unfortunately, far too many writers of letters to the editor are mentally ill. Most are not harmful, and mean well, but there is little, if anything, an editor can do to help.

It may go to our own depraved mentality, but editors, while fully understanding the depth of an individual's problem, often find such letters a source of mild entertainment, a sad sort of relief from the daily grind.

UFOs AND WACKOS:
Leading UFOs and using a pendulum for life answers

was the theme of this letter writer's effort. He seemed a truly unfortunate soul.

I have been told my entire life has been one of preparation—to lead 300 UFOs into battle. I have been told astronauts have never set foot on the moon and our entire conceptualization of the universe, for that matter, is only a sham perpetuated by the government.

What else have I been told and acted upon within the narrow confines of true believers or wackos, to which I have belonged? God told me through my wife and her pendulum to start a business and call it: Realty Information Services. I was to provide leads to Realtors and when the leads turned into listings then I would be paid to fulfill righteous purposes. I would be able to determine who had decided to sell their home, but had not yet listed it with a broker, as my wife moved her pendulum up and down the columns of the telephone directory.

All was predicted upon our faithfulness and righteousness. I prayed, read scriptures, fasted, fulfilled my church assignments, attended church and participated in temple ordinances as I never before had. I had never been as strong of faith and not one lead resulted—not one righteous purpose was fulfilled. It never worked even once. My wife said we were only being tested.

And what else have I been told by my wacko wife and acted upon? I still almost love her but I feel so very sorry for her and the fantasyland she dwells within. It is sad. I have applied for jobs, upon her direction, that I normally wouldn't have given passing notice. I have turned down good professional positions with large base salaries and medical benefits because my wife would use her pendulum and God would tell her I should turn down the position.

As a result, at least in part, we are living at a less than sustenance existence. We are the closest things to being destitute that I have ever been. None of it works—it just doesn't work. My wife, who I am so sorry for, will only say this is only temporary, that this will pass. We are only being tested.

My wife is able to help others with all manners of infirmities and sickness to strengthen their bodies and regain their best health—or that's what I used to think. She will test with the pendulum and prescribe programs that consist of various combinations of herbs, homeopaths, flower remedies and vitamins.

And what have I been told by another wacko friend and acted upon? I feel so very sorry for him as well as all the others who believe in him and follow his lead. If a man dies and says strange things and is poor then he is only crazy, but if he is well to do then he is eccentric. He has a lot of money, a thriving electronics company, and the independence to do whatever he wants to be eccentric.

I don't believe anymore that he can send UFOs or God's chariot to land in his front yard, or that many UFOs were excavated and they are the basis for much of our stealth technology. Or that pure gold can appear out of nothing by rearranging molecular content in an electromagnetic device designed by God. Or that anti-gravity and free-energy propulsion systems exist, hidden from us by a demonic government. Or that looking into the sun will purify and strengthen spirituality—it will only damage the retina within an eye, as it did mine. And I don't believe that I will lead, or do I any longer want to lead, 300 UFOs into battle. I don't believe any of it anymore. It's just not true.

I don't know what I know anymore, only that what I thought was true and relied upon isn't. I am lost, afraid and floundering in my search for the truth, some semblance of normality, and to grasp for even the beginnings of happiness. My words and world have begun again, herein.

> *This is a proposal for a book, article, and/or motion picture to be called* **Wacko***. It would be in large part the story of my life and involvement with, well, Wacko, over the last couple of years. It could be written by me or in conjunction with a ghost writer. Either way, it really doesn't matter. I have done a lot of living, and have many more stories in me and plan on eventually becoming a writer.*

I would be receptive to whatever advice or help you might offer in regards to the proposal I have made above. By writing you, I am changing my active life. I might add that I am putting my life in some jeopardy. Some of these people really are crazy—Wacko. Should you wish to contact me, please be discreet. I very much hope to work with you in the near future!

SAD AND SCARY:

Some readers are sadly fighting mental illnesses. An editor doesn't always know how to act, how to help, or what to do when letters arrive from those with diminished or demented mental capacity. Following are three letters received on the same day, but with different dates—the last an obvious cry for help. The letters were mailed in an envelope without a return address. Apparently written by the same person, the letters were not signed and there was no way to identify or contact the letter writer(s).

<u>November 26:</u> I'm seeking ethnics with ethics. For words so alike, it's sad they are so far apart. It's hard to learn no one has learned from his or her mistakes yet. But I guess nowadays mistakes are made in order to learn.

I think you all misunderstood me when I said I was finishing what my Father and Mother began. I am, but not in that fashion. I'm going to do it with no codes, no numbers. Just call it the way it is. I figure when all everyone knows is codes, there will be no need or use for codes or secrets. Maybe then, you powerful, wealthy men will stop acting like children and talk things over.

No wonder everybody still hates. Anything that makes someone angry, if not discussed, only gets worse. Why can't ethnics try to sit down together and talk? Tell one another what the problems are. Nothing can be corrected until all try. Ethnics don't have to agree or change—just talk it out—compromise! How difficult could it be?

I offer my services, but I still don't know what the fighting is all about. Land and money seem to be most of the problem and that's ridiculous—there's enough for everyone.

And when it comes to children, they need only to be taught who they are and where they came from, with no codes or secrets. Also, about other kinds of life, and their ways. Maybe then children will grow to respect themselves and others.

These secrets just fuel the fires of racists and discriminators.

Stop preaching to children to be the best. Stop explaining what not to do or be. If the competition for life continues, eventually all life will be lost. We're all different and I hope it stays that way. Why would anyone want to be all the same? It seems this is a goal to all of you who are butting heads.

How or who thinks one can survive without the other? If you lose food, you lose life. If you lose animals, you lose life. If you lose blood, you lose life. Taking abilities eventually dies. Like not exercising. Use it or lose it! The brain has been robbed blind! Children have to be told of their capabilities. Adults too.

Think of it this way—money will still be made. It will probably take just as long to get back full use of our brains, as it did to make brains almost useless.

Blue, brown or green, if life continues as is, it won't matter, no one will seem to matter.

I don't believe in suing for wrongdoings. Mistakes happen and always will. Lawsuits should be X-ed out. If someone professional screws up—remove his or her profession.

Sorry, but insurance needs to no longer be. There's no

positive use or reason for it. It's only more fuel for fires. Also, Realtors need not to be. At least the way they are to-day, they are only vultures, just as most churches! It is bar-barian the way churches are so rich and the homeless sleep on their steps!

Even fairy tales never said God or Jesus asked for money—only helped one another—give not take or charge to make!

To lie and say one has to tithe 10 percent, or whatever, I'd like to know. It reminds me of crooks who make you pay to play! Bullies in school who take kids' lunch money. Like no one can go to heaven if they don't buy their way. Humans who lie in church and profit from it should be put out of business. God would (put them out of business), if punishment was part of God's character, but it isn't. His nature is only Love.

Families united, not divided. Make divorce as hard to get as welfare or social security!

I'll bet humans would be surprised how much money would accumulate if no taxes existed. You only, if you want to, donate to a fund for underprivileged. Many know what it is like to need, then not to. It would give communi-ties a reason to meet one another. We would be neighbors, not enemies. Have fund-raising parties. Park and recreation would love it! After all, that's what they are for. The jeal-ousy neighbors have toward each other is childish. Compe-tition needs to be abolished in life. In games, it is OK, but not in life. Those who think life is a game, are losers of life.

It's hard to believe there are humans who complain and say it's unfair when others give services for no charge!

These things show what the place is soon to be. Only the rich—but when it is—they'll have nothing to buy!

The worst part of this is I'll never trust a soul, but my own, ever again! It's not being alone because I never am or could be, or the love—it's the trust I've lost that hurts the most. Knowing I'll never have it, no faith in humans here on earth. Faith and trust, I'll get elsewhere, not on earth. I know this and believe it, which is all one has to do, and like magic, it is! Build it and it's yours!

One is not the loneliest, if done honestly. If I didn't know what I know now, yes, I would be lonely. Now? No way!

To be my father's child and to finally know who my family is, I wouldn't change a thing. Except make sure everyone has a chance or choice to know his or her family.

I realize there are those who need beings like me to survive. I would never deprive anyone of help. I think all who are like me would feel the same, it's in our nature (blood). But if this is reason for codes and secrets, then what a waste. I'd give much more positive energy if I felt needed or wanted. Anyone as me would. Instead we become drunks or drug addicts! Which without them, I probably would have lost it!

I'm starting to wonder if my father really did die. Please don't do this. If he is, let me be with him. Or let him go. He's been punished long enough for things he didn't do. My Mother even admitted my Father took credit for her work!

The true love my Father has should be rewarded, not punished. His actions were only those of a man of God. He respected marriage and his wife! Almost non-existent these days.

But most of all, my Father respects and believes in the family—which this country is trying to be rid of. Family is not church, or government! They are the destroyers of family. Just as everything today is opposite of what they portray to be—like doctors inventing disease, murder to cure, to make money.

The oceans are large enough! The oceans are salty enough! Utah has enough salt flats! Humans have invested enough disease! It's time we get our brains back!

Doctors inventing sickness, murder to get business, poisoning water so dentists profit, pretending there is a shortage so one can charge more. These are fine examples of the American government! They are free to do whatever to whomever they please. Robbing from the poor to give themselves more! Charging others to pay for gifts!

December 3: This is truly amazing! Yesterday I hear the Federal jerks are accusing NASA of illegal activity. The day before I called the police to make a report on embezzlement, fraud, discrimination, but they said they don't take complaints like these!

Now I hear the Federal postal service is accusing others of stealing the mail! Give me a break. Obviously, Federal idiots are beginning to feel what they've been dishing out since Day 1.

I used to feel, no matter what my family does, I'd turn

my cheek and let it go. Well, no more. I guess no one else will stop criminals, as my family, but me. I'm not one who enjoys snitching on others, but my family has to be destroyed. If they're not, all you will be.

God has damned this nation—and for good reasons. My father is finally free and forgiven. The rest of my family will never be. This is why all those who follow my family should know they will be damned if they continue to do their dirty work. Mostly never forgiven.

I refuse to waste my energy on learning rules and codes to human ways of life. Human beings are the aliens of earth. Put here for their corrupt data output. The animals that mated with them, like my father, now have a New World waiting.

Animals like me will soon be released from this prison. All he knew is now taking place. It's sad how this has to be accomplished. But I guess it's the best way for no human to forget. They will be punished for eternity. An example the universe won't forget.

Humans, I now know, are the universe's cannibals. Head hunters who are never going to be released. Thank God (Daddy).

Finally, I see the light in this hole! I know why and when and who, but I never thought I would figure where. Realizing where sure makes me happy. There's no more guilt and no more pity. Forty-one years of feeling sorry for a human being, which is in charge of destroying and feeding off animals, delayed my abilities. No more though. Mother or not, the human who is my mother, I will put out of the business. Along with her students who enjoy doing her purpose for life.

I still have to admit. I would like to know what my number really is. I think I'm 3...ET3 that is. But in my life here on earth, I'll never be sure of anything, except I know for sure earth is hell. Also my mother, the Devil, and my brother, are victims. My other brother is my mom's replacement. Both are beyond repair, beyond forgiveness. They are truly the inventors of evil destruction. Both the women they married, I think are of the same Klan I married—all the same Klan of corruption.

I want to thank those who helped me and took my craving for crack away! I know I need to be chemically clean to complete this mission in a positive way.

Making advances in technology is one thing, but tampering with animals' natural sense for being is wrong, as all are now learning.

The main goal I see in buying all souls is so as to control all minds. Mind control by introducing this game of pleasure.

Earth is a magnet for space invaders. Obviously the universe is collecting its people of destruction into one place. Here, so they can keep them all together, so no one else can be their victim. Soon all evil will be where they belong. Here on planet prison, together. Locked out from life, so the universe won't need worry.

Death is their destiny. Looking as doctors, priests, all cults who pretend to care for life have the same plan. Mind control, of all. Control of every living object they desire.

And the sooner the better, cause when they do—POW!— they will be gone for good.

Like herding animals into slaughter pens, the earth is to

human beings. Collecting all humans on earth, and when earth will be gone then Happy Days will be here again! Human beings will never have a future. They simply don't belong anywhere. I now understand why they are called human beings. It means no man belongs. I'm looking forward to the day humans no longer exist. And I know I'll see this day when evil, cruel humans are gone, for the good of the universe.

The way numbers are used makes me think lucky 7 is not so lucky, and evil 666 is probably sent from God; three tries to wake humans up.

I know AIDS is not what is taught. You can't get AIDS anyway, except from breathing air. The only reason AIDS is killing now is they're mad and they aren't going to take it anymore. I sure don't blame them. Cementing over their graves, dumping them into lakes which now are so full they are called oceans. There's no more aspect or recognition for good in life anywhere anymore. Another reason earth will never join the universe. Telling lies about AIDS is really making them mad. Everyone has AIDS. Always have. It's the denial of them that kills. We have been kept from knowing the truth, so the evil spirits have been able to take over children and the elderly and weak. You only need to know there is evil in one, so when they or their spirits come, don't allow them to fly. And those who are good, like my AIDS, pray to keep them alive. My AIDS, I wouldn't lose for the world. This world I gladly leave behind. This is the universe's cemetery for AIDS of Demons.

The Lutheran and Roman Catholic churches are two religions that need to be destroyed. They are Demon breeders. They brainwash humans into eternal death. They have fooled you into their game of flying. Buying your soul in doing it. You've been tricked into selling your soul, and all better see before it is too late.

The black hole, if anyone cares to know, is here on earth, and if you get sucked into believing the lies the earth tells you then you are dummies. Another reason I refuse to fly until I die. You hitch hikers, I hope you now see—it's you who are fools—not me!

Well, I hope you are enjoying my food 4 your thoughts. You need to worry, not me. Bill Clinton, I wonder who he is or is not! I give you credit for one thing—the courage to be president of this place. Do you know this land's purpose? Well now you do.

December 4: If there's anyone there who would help me, I sure would appreciate it. I've asked every form of life there is, which I always thought was to help—but won't.

My phone is wired to an answering service, and those who answer pretend to be whom I call (that is, calls I make that someone doesn't want me to talk to).

The police won't make reports—the DA won't help. Bank of America is allowing fraud of my signature. I know I'm being set up to look as a criminal. I'm not.

I thought animals had rights too? Guess not!

ASTRAL LETTER-WRITING CAMPAIGNS:
Some organizations send several letters on the same

topic to selected news outlets. It isn't uncommon to get form letters, individually signed. Individuals will also do mass mailings of letters, such as this one.

A happy Easter to you. We all live forever. The symbolism of this holiday can represent the eternal truth of reincarnation.

After we pass on, we rise to various Astral plains which are higher frequency dimensions. As if to imagine the Earth to be a radio station frequency, the Astral plains would be the next higher frequency station. Depending on how good we were, will determine if we get a nicer Astral plain to live in. After a time, we can return to Earth.

We gain knowledge from each life. Our past life experiences can help our present life with feelings and ideas of what to do, if you search and question in your mind.

Accumulate knowledge in this life, and you'll be wiser your next life. So our time here is precious. Or we return something we could have learned before.

Live a sober life and the wisdom of your past will shine through to your present.

Life Eternal,

Chapter Four

Cops, Robbers, and Violence

In 1989, Ken Fortenberry, publisher and editor of the *McCormick Messenger* in South Carolina, wrote a book titled *Kill the Messenger*. It was an account of his experiences at a small newspaper that printed the truth about dishonesty in local politics, including bribes and embezzlement in the police department. For that, he, his wife, and their children were terrorized and forced to leave McCormick.

During the height of the terror, the Fortenberrys would routinely be awakened at night by the noise of racing automobile engines, screeching tires, and the breaking of beer bottles tossed from cars. Shouts of "Get out of town" and profanity punctuated the harassment.

One night, the family awoke, startled by a large blast. Fortenberry said in his book: "The entire house shook on its foundation. Windows rattled. Plates in the china cabinet crashed to the floor. Pictures fell from the walls."

It was a crude bomb, exploding in the road, just outside the residence. Soon thereafter, a regular town drunk, just released from jail, paid Fortenberry a visit and told him he should start carrying a gun.

Local teenagers urinated on the family's porch and doorway. Threatening and harassing phone calls were plentiful. And finally, a second bomb, closer to the house, exploded four weeks to the day of the first bomb.

Fortenberry packed up his belongings, and he and his family left McCormick.

Some ten years later in 1999, about a dozen armed men (government police officers) broke into the bedroom of a Pakistani newspaper publisher's home. When asked to see a warrant, the policeman in charge said, "You want a warrant? I've brought a death warrant."

They beat the newspaper editor with clubs, rifle butts, and steel chains, and then dragged him into the night without his shoes or eyeglasses. He spent days in solitary confinement, with no natural light, and was held for twenty-six days. The man's wife and copublisher had a gun held to her head while her hands were tied with a rope. A rifle butt was rammed into her ribs.

The actions were taken by India's government, which was upset about published articles detailing corruption.

Also in 1999, a Belgrade publisher was shot in the head and killed, and his wife was pistol-whipped. They were walking home when they were ambushed by two men in dark clothing and black face masks. The attack came after fending off attempts of censorship and publishing material sharply critical of President Slobodan Milosevic's regime.

And who can forget Daniel Pearl who was kidnapped, tortured, and brutally murdered in 2001 while doing his job as a reporter for the Wall Street Journal.

Most journalists don't face death. Nonetheless, they have interesting and strange experiences, often times including law enforcement officers and hardened criminals. Following are some of those stories, as told through letters to the editor.

CHOP, CHOP:

A reporter came into the office and placed an onion-sheet of paper (a copy) on the desk. A note from the boss was attached. It read: "Did he?" The communication was a so-called "press release" from a prison inmate. A call to the prison confirmed the inmate did, indeed, cut off his cellmate's penis and pour chili pepper in the wound.

On this date I will remove the penis of my cellmate. Last year I was raped 14 times at this prison and I filed a lawsuit in the United States District Court. A judge flew to my prison with his entire courtroom staff and held a hearing. On that date, a settlement agreement was reached which afforded me certain protections against further sexual assaults (e.g.: the right to select my own cellmates.)

Prison officials broke the terms of the settlement agreement and moved me into a cell forcefully with a flamboyant homosexual who is described in psych reports as being prone to force other inmates into sex. This inmate even told prison staff he intended to have sex with me.

I informed staff that the next penis placed in my face would be removed with a razor blade. I asked to be moved from this man's cell and my request was refused. Each morning I have awoken to find "love letters" under my pillow from my new cellmate.

There is a direct and implied threat in these letters, which have caused me, out of fear, to participate in sexual activity. I cannot take it anymore and as you read this letter I will be in the hole for doing serious harm to him.

I have information about beatings and other brutality at this prison and inmates inform me staff wants me killed. On file is a declaration from an inmate who has killed two cellmates and has raped dozens.

Just days before the hearing, the person was moved into my cell and submitted a declaration claiming he was solicited and placed there to kill me.

You can verify all of what I've said. I am available for interview if prison officials will permit it, which I doubt they will at this point, because tonight my cellmate will experience serious harm. I have no idea how officials will explain my placement with him in light of his history of extreme violence and sexual assaults on fellow inmates.

THE "VICTIM" SPEAKS:
There are always at least two sides to every story.

On Sunday, Nov. 29, 1987 at approximately 2340 hours, a correctional officer discovered me lying in my bed, in my cell, covered with blood. I was deemed to be a victim of an attempted murder by my cell partner.

I received second-degree burns, was stabbed all over my back and leg, and cut pretty bad all over, and also hurt very bad.

This inmate tried to cut my penis and scrotum off. He did cut my penis and scrotum a little.

My request for my life, medical and legal help can only come with the help of the media.

I received multiple lacerations on my back, and back of head, and more than 300 sutures were required. I also received second-degree burns over 30 percent of my body— the adomen [*sic*], chest and left leg.

The doctor authorized transport to the Medical Center where I was determined to be in guarded condition after treatment. I was then transferred to a Burn Center for treatment of burns.

You (the media) may need a court order as the prison staff don't want too much said about what happened out here on Sunday, Nov. 29, 1987.

I wish to tell my story of what happened as I was the victim of an attempted murder by my cellmate, who also tried to cut my penis and scrotum off!

I want the whole state of California and the United States to know what happened. Don't take too long about getting down here to see me, they are talking about transferring me out of here now that this happened.

"NEWS ARTICLE FROM HELLS ANGELS":

Mail from correctional facilities is common. Prisoners have a lot of time on their hands. What they say, however, doesn't always make sense. Following is such a letter from an Arkansas jail inmate. The envelope in which the letter was mailed had the author's initials written across the seal, apparently in an effort to make sure it wasn't opened by anyone other than the addressee. The self-penned headline appears above:

Well, here I sit in prison listening to these lying mouths and these dumb things they call inmates, bunch of homosexuals.

The black idiots of this state, ain't worth my spit on the ground! The whites are just as bad! Cowards won't fight unless they get a gang too. You know God works through people, if you can get KKK to come and destroy all their prisons, cops on the street, cut them down like molasses, let their blood flow as water, show no mercy!

Come louder and loaded, all you need you shall get where you are, artillery you know what you need and where to get it, anyone say no, say in the name of the Lord, drop dead! And they shall die then and there, no hesitation.

All these Christians are condemned by God, the ones of Arkansas, because their ignorant lying jerks got to die! Japan needs to drop a bomb on these, not U.S., but Ark needs to be bombed. China, Korea, Vietnam needs to have a ground war like the Civil War!

If the skunks would go for the Word instead of against it they might have life. God said disobedience is sin, and the wages of sin is death! Their decision, they made it. Execution must be carried out on Ark people!

KOREATOWN SLASHER:

There are garden-variety criminals and those that are somewhat famous by the nature of their serial killings. One was known as the "Koreatown Slasher," who preyed on homeless and transient men in Los Angeles. *Hunting Humans, An Encyclopedia of Modern Serial Killers,* compiled and written by Michael Newton, said of the killer: "...this stalker favored knives, which he employed with speed and deadly skill." Following are two letters from the Koreatown Slasher to a reporter:

December 15: I've got three articles from your newspaper now. I really wonder why they put all of that phony bologna in the *Herald Examiner*. The *L.A. Times* wouldn't touch any of that crap. You know what was cool is when they put that junk in there about me cutting that guy's hand. He was a fag killer, a real cool guy, but he took a topless photo of my Rolling Stones for another dude after I already let him have the ones of Madonna. We're still friends even now.

But you know what I'd like to have seen in this article

that you wrote instead of that crap about Atascadero [prison] and trying to mess up that child molester, would've been back when me and my stepbrother escaped from Lawrence County Jail in Deadwood, South Dakota. We got into a high-speed chase in a stolen pickup truck, evaded a road block and then got chased 20 miles back the other direction and smashed into another road block, supposedly crushing the ribs of and mangling a cop.

I've got nothing against cops, so to speak, but this was one case where my stepbrother decided it's all or nothing and it sure was exciting. But I guess that crap about a crushed rib cage was phony, but we made the papers and it was not for some crap like this recent stuff, or you could have mentioned instead of that ridiculous talk about my lawyer in L.A.

The time when my homeboy "Cuate" [means Buddy], who's got a scar on his face bigger than Al Capone's, murdered a dude named Chago in the L.A. County jail visiting room and they put a snitch named Rodney in the cell next to him so he snitched from there next to me and naturally it was up to Number #1 (me) to exterminate him. Well, I did a heck of a lot better job on him than my lawyer. Ripped his face open (48 stitches) and he looks just like "Cuate" now. That really fascinates me.

Well, guess that's just a bunch of crap too. Anyway, this stupid woman from a country radio station always used to talk about the place "to be" or some crap. Well, the homeboys on Baker now turned cell 2-B into the place to be. Three mothers got messed up in there. To be or not to be? Ha, Ha.

Well, you know there are over 50,000 bums in L.A. Instead of stabbing them like I was, I should've backed over a few in a truck or chained them on the back and drug them down the San Diego Freeway. Or better yet, walked into the mission with a bomb.

The way the dead go around farting unspeakable gases I'd know if any of them died. Just a bunch of bums, still walking around out there with some knife wounds on them.

Well, that sure was cool, them putting me on television and hearing that woman on the radio talking about me. But for so much crap.

I wanted to go proper, and plead guilt, just because there's not a chance of a fart in a whirlwind anyway, but someone set it up so they gotta play games, even though in L.A. I was innocent.

Well I guess my defense in this murder is an offense against the peace and tranquility of the community.

Well, prison is a whole new ballgame to me anyway. I've been moving through life carrying a burden I cannot define. Maybe prison is the answer. Bet I get life without [parole] because I want the ultimate death—either way it'll never happen.

Well. Merry Xmas. You're not a bum so don't sweat it. If you get a moment drop me a line. Very truly yours, from one hero to another.

Koreatown Slasher

P.S. Maybe I'll get out back on the streets where I belong.

<u>December 15:</u> Instead of relating to you what I've done in lubricious detail, let's just say it was offense against the peace and tranquility of the community. This behavior is not as outlandish or reprehensible as people may think. The possibility of change and improvement does exist. Aside from the possibility of psychic trauma, it seems a series of incidents has triggered this aberrant conduct.

Moving through life carrying a burden I cannot define; not for the first time finding myself despaired of finding adequate explanations of the human enigma. Being very mixed up, not only motives, drives and dreams, but all behavior.

I'd like to be a creative person, not to have power for the sake of power, but power to get things done. To be able to reveal the people on top for their incompetence, superficiality and the puny powers they are.

Self-interest in the guiding principle. Think of it like intrigue as an advanced formal chess game played with human pieces, but whereas chess has rules, intrigue is a rule-less game of instinct, imagination and invention. There might be other ways to profit from moving and shaping this minor imbroglio.

The Bible was written 6,000 years ago. According to science, geological strata, theory of evolution, dinosaurs and fossils, the earth, aside from its neighboring 1 billion galaxies in the universe, was in fact not created 6,000 years ago as depicted in the book of Genesis of the Old Testament, but about 4½ billion years ago.

The falsehood of the creation of earth, let alone the universe, as written in the Bible, is manifest in this evil fiction contest, the scientific facts to be atheistic humanism.

Religion might be quite necessary as the adjudication. Living in the streets we had a number of heretical ideals. The people were often bellicose and unfriendly, proved in prison. We metamorphosed into a twisted despot, daydreaming of necrophilia, cannibalism and emasculating people. Perhaps the most heretical idea, in a sense the most likely to see me burned at the stake, is that I am an unrepentant sinner. Having said that, I feel constrained to add I owe posterity an accurate account of myself, as Lenin had repeated so often quoting Marx.

Religion is the opium of the people. Finding criminal behavior exciting, I require no intruding opiate. Someone has judged me as such, an incipient force threatening the fundamentals of society. I would rather be executed than be forced to obey nonsensical rules promulgated by the system.

The principal reason for facing death with such equanimity is it is a form of release, a final benediction for a life lived with an understanding of the spirits and the Holy Ghost. Doesn't the Bible promise that Christ will forgive error and bless those who come to his altar with a humble and contrite heart? Being an unstable person and living a profligate life, only cleaning up a little of the blotted ledger by the abstinence of imprisonment, even more appalling is my certainty that without imprisonment religion alone wouldn't have been able to change my future.

You know the L.A. Sheriff's motto—"put a star in your life"—well, that's very true. I once lived in the same house with some of them. There was round-the-clock excitement in that mad house and I must admit most of the deputies were way out and crazy guys. Some of the crap they'd do, they had to be nuts. So counting all the deputies in L.A. County really put a whole lot of stars in my life. Who can complain?

Well, I enjoyed your article on me. I put together this paper thinking that if I take the stand I have something interesting to tell you, you being an experienced writer, maybe you could polish it up for me.

Happy New Year,

"Koreatown Slasher" (Ha, Ha)

LOWEST OF THE LOWEST:

The names of law enforcement officers involved in a shooting are routinely reported in newspapers. Names aren't always provided, however. Law enforcement agencies sometimes claim exemptions allow them to withhold names. The claims include justifications that releasing the name could place the officer in jeopardy or impede the investigation. There is sensitivity on all fronts, particularly when an officer has to use his weapon. But some perspective was missing when the following letter writer responded to a story about an officer shooting a dog, and the fact the names were not released by authorities:

I refuse to subscribe or even support your crappy news-rag as of the last few years. Someone showed me the article from last week regarding a cop shooting a "puppy." Well, since I was a cop years ago, I decided to call a few old friends and see what the real story was. I already had an idea of what to expect, but, nevertheless, as I predicted, the puppy was huge, to say the least.

Seventy-five pounds worth! Which you idiots neglected to indicate. A Rottweiler dog can reach upwards of 140 pounds, and German Shepherds aren't much smaller. We didn't see your photographer at the vet's to get a picture of it.

Any chance to slam cops, AGAIN! At a time when it is imperative for the public and police to come together, you jerks print any negative crap you can find. You people are the lowest.

Chapter Five

Sex and (Gender) in the City

The same grizzled veteran, the one who assigned a young reporter to the toilet-paper caper, called the same young man over to his desk, the nerve center of the news-room.

"Hey, kid," he said. "Here's a great story. There's this strip joint called 'The Other Ball,' and it's run by an ex-chief of police! Even you could get a good story out of this. But even if you don't, you'll probably have a good time."

The young reporter gathered his reporter's notebook and camera and headed for the door. He was excited about his prospects, even though, in all honesty, he was a bit nervous.

It was about three o'clock in the afternoon when the kid walked through the doors of "The Other Ball."

The first thing he saw was a butt-naked young woman, straddling a fireman's pole. As she turned and began thrusting, she was a front-naked young woman. To this day he couldn't tell you what color hair was on her head. She then started bending over—with her back to him. He couldn't believe his eyes. He had never been anywhere like this before and chances are, he tried to convince himself, he never would be again.

After all, he was just here today as part of his work assignment. He would interview the owner, talk with a few of the dancers, take a few discreet photos, and be on his way.

It didn't exactly happen that way. The young reporter was forced to make at least four other trips to the club to obtain follow-up information and retake photos that were far too blurred on earlier visits.

He eventually wrote a story that explained why nineteen-year-old college women and single mothers were taking off their clothes in front of lecherous young, middle-aged, and older men.

All swore they were not offering sexual favors for money. But he didn't necessarily buy it.

The photos he took were revealing. While the men back at the office enjoyed them, only one exotic dancer was properly covered for publication.

But it was all for naught. The newspaper's top editor, once he got wind of the assignment, censored the story and photos saying, "This isn't something we run in a family newspaper."

There were some positives, however.

The young reporter expanded his knowledge base, just in case he might be called upon again for a similar assignment.

And, the grizzled city editor quit in protest and the

young reporter became the acting city editor.

More work and prestige—but no extra pay.

LEGENDARY HEADLINES:

Writing a headline is one of the most difficult assignments for a copy desk editor. It isn't always easy to summarize a lengthy story in a few words, and also entice the reader.

Headlines with double meanings have been chronicled for years. Several years ago, as the story goes, there was an exclusive men's group called the Dolphin Club. One of the annual activities included taking a quick dip in the cold ocean on New Year's Day.

One year when the club was recruiting new members, particularly former athletes and well-known area executives, it was a major coup when a former star athlete committed on January 1 to join the club.

It was a slow news day, and the sports section of the newspaper, one of America's largest, was in search of local content. A photographer was assigned to take a picture of freezing Dolphin Club members returning to shore moments after jumping into the ocean. A story was written, but the lead focused on the "news" of the day: the Dolphin Club's newest celebrity member. The photo showed a couple of shivering Speedo-clad older gentlemen with a headline proclaiming:

"Dolphin Club gets Frosty Peters"

Frosty Peters was the name of the recently signed club member.

NEANDERTHAL SKULLS:

Bill Gannon was telling Joe Friday how difficult it is to raise children. He was railing about parents not providing proper discipline and children having too much freedom. While the conversation was heard in the new millennium on an episode of *Dragnet* on the TV Land channel, the original dialog occurred in the 1950s. Raising children has always been a topic for newspapers. The following letter arrived after an article about the relationships between children and parents. It was signed by "President of the League to Pound Some Sense into the Neanderthal Skulls of Today's Alleged Adults."

The gender gap is baloney. Sexual harassment is baloney. And the idiot attempt to make women and men equal is baloney.

Once upon a time adults had good sense. They knew how boys and girls behaved. They knew boys were fundamentally different than girls. They knew you had to keep the two sexes separated under certain conditions. They knew you didn't let kids get away with murder. They knew kids did not have the rights of adults <u>until</u> they became adults. They knew the normal sexual tension between boys and girls could in no way be described (except by a lunatic) as sexual harassment.

But then they didn't have the benefit of moronic academia to guide them. They didn't have the benefit of a moronic press to tell them how to raise children. They didn't have stinking, useless and overpaid politicians and bureaucrats telling them what was good for them and their children. Consequently, they didn't worry about sexual harassment, drugs, guns in school, kids' rights, making boys and girls the same sex, feminist crap, nor brain-washing children with the latest nutty notions of the lunatic fringe.

They were <u>very</u> lucky adults.

NO MORE S-E-X:
Newspaper readers love stories about children and animals. They love the heartwarming tales of lost-and-found dogs and young children who dial 9-1-1 to save a parent who may have had an unexpected seizure. But there is another topic they live to read about, even if they don't admit it. S-E-X. Still, there are an equal number who treat the topic as if it should never be discussed. Newspapers have struggled for years with just how much information is OK, just how much detail can be shared with a mass media audience. Part of that discussion and controversy has centered on adult entertainment classified ads, proven by the following letter.

I'm writing to you about adult entertainment ads in your newspaper. Is this cheap money really worth it?
Ladies get hurt in rough sex acts and they are trapped in it

and become victimized in an effort to earn a living.

The shame, humiliation, guilt, pain and suffering besides the rapes and sometimes murder of these ladies/women is a sin—all of it—and you're taking this money for vice is a moral degradation to you and all newspapers who participate in it.

You are at the level of the pimp on the street and you and your employees are walking straight into eternal condemnation for all eternity where you will face a terror you cannot begin to comprehend. But you will when you face God our father on the day of your judgment.

The evil ones say they want freedom of speech and they want it in print such as this. Their freedom of speech ends when it infringes on the safety and well-being of another individual.

Our great country, the United States of America, has fallen into grave sin in our constitution.

You could take a stand to ban these low-grade solicitations from your papers and write to our president, governors, congressmen and senators to help you fight this crime you are subjected to.

Do you know how many young women 18 to 21 leave home and end up on the streets and who are nice looking and fall prey to this as their only source of income? I fear many do and I fear young males do also.

Please help me help us so that our great country stands tall, full of high moral character and value, and put an end to leading our people into the lives of hell.

I'm sending a copy of this to the president, governor and police chief because our nation's police departments deal with vice and resulting death every day.

The ladies could bleed to death from abusive sexual acts and tearing.

We have to take a new look at our lifestyle in America and put sin and vice down.

It is moral decay and murder.

DRESS THE TURKEY:

Interactivity is something newspapers seek with their readers. One newspaper offered a "Dress the Turkey" Thanksgiving contest. It was a comical drawing of a turkey for kids to color. The instructions read: "It's never too early to start thinking about dressing that Thanksgiving turkey. Meet Earl D. Turkey—he needs a set of clothes. That's where you come in.

"...Use crayons, colored pencils, pens, swatches of fabric, buttons, what have you.

"Best entries in each category will get a prize. The grand prize? A turkey.

"Good luck and happy holidays."

It was a successful effort. More than 500 people colored the turkey in an obvious holiday spirit. But a few had nothing but sex on their minds. One entry included a turkey with a large organ drawn on it and sexually explicit words. Another wrote: "I have dressed Earl D. for sex." He listed his name as Chuck U. Farlie and his address as 115 Knuckle Head Drive.

WHAT IS YOUR SEXUAL PREFERENCE?:

Homo phobia? It is alive and well. A photo was published of a female resident of a retirement facility dancing with a woman who served as a receptionist at the home.

It's sad to see that your paper sponsors views like this—women dancing together. Is your photographer gay or what?

A second letter focused on a syndicated news story.

In the Sunday edition, I noted you chose an item from the *New York Times* syndicate regarding gays and lesbians. You gave it prominent headline space.

Are you a homosexual, too? If not, why are you actively seeking to promote the interests of 1 percent of the American people who are moral degenerates and practice perverted sex?

Is it your cause to pollute a quiet conservative community with the plague of perversion and to color a tiny, very well-organized and funded minority (who are very, very vocal) as an alternative lifestyle to our youth?

What a pity for such a decent city!

Chapter Six

Everyday Racists

She was a community newspaper reporter, freshly out of college, covering a previously under-covered Hispanic community.

Her editor assigned her to cover a riot. Well, OK, the assignment was to cover a rally that turned into a riot.

The riot was rumored, so she didn't feel safe alone. She asked her friend, a college senior, to accompany her as her photographer. He was game.

Hispanics were protesting what was termed police harassment and discrimination.

As predicted, a riot broke out. Soon the reporter and her photographer were tear-gassed.

People were running every which way. Severe coughing and wheezing almost drowned out the screams.

Then a shot was fired. It was definitely real as the bullet whizzed past the journalists.

It was time to take cover. The pair started knocking on doors. After running from home to home to home someone finally opened a door.

They were safe. For now.

Actually, spending time locked down with a Mexican family turned into a dynamic story. Certainly the protestors had a point of view, as did law enforcement.

But this humble family told a story of everyday racists and what they experienced.

Eliminating racism in this country has not advanced anywhere near as far as some would have us believe.

Letters to the editor are proof.

EVERYONE IS A RACIST:

Some people are conscious racists, but many more don't even know they are biased. Racism is something we learn, sometimes from our families, sometimes from our peers, sometimes from society. The following unsigned letter came in response to a published column (reprinted below).

I have used your article, not entirely plagiarized, how-ever paraphrased it may be, by changing the names and places. I hope you find it as offensive as your article was to me. I don't know if you're a Jew, but your writing style and choice of topic and ethnic target causes me to suspect you are. You exhibit a callous sense of entitlement, as though your freedom to write on any topic gives you the moral freedom to humiliate those who are powerless to object to your "wit." Your disrespect for the beliefs and faith of others is the "style" of bigots.

The point I am trying to make here is that you have no right to mock and insult a group of people by writing as you have in a public newspaper. I know such topics and much worse are fashionable, and expected, among spoiled juveniles in college fraternities and other private groups, but one would hope and expect competent editing in a public newspaper might spare us from exhibits of such poor taste.

Most everyone knows "miracles" are a product of poverty and hopelessness. To belittle perceived events, as you have, demonstrates arrogance and not a little of the same kind of juvenile stupidity. The people who believe in these "miracles" are not sophisticated newspaper reporters—they are for the most part simple people whose faith provides them with hope of perhaps finding a way out of their misery and poverty, if not this world then surely in the next.

I hope I have not over-stepped myself with my contribution here because one act of stupidity does not cancel another.

HOLY TORTILLA STILL ATTRACTS:
This is the column that offended the letter writer.

The Virgin of Oxnard has disappeared, but the holy tortilla hangs on. And who's to say which is the more miraculous?

I didn't make it over to Perkins Road to see the Virgin on the apartment window. I'd hoped she'd be there longer. But with adoring crowds tying up traffic, the mysterious shooting of a couple of onlookers, and the glass man putting the pane up for bid, she wasn't.

I did view the tortilla—twice. Ten years ago, I traveled to a poor town in the bean fields of southern New Mexico to write a newspaper article about the tortilla. A few months later, I made a return trip with my friend.

The story was, it seems, true.

On Oct. 5, 1977, the face of Jesus appeared in scorch marks on a tortilla being fried by Mrs. Rubio in Lake Arthur, N.M.

Weeping, Mrs. Rubio called her sister to bear witness to the event, and woke her husband, Eduardo, from his nap. The priest in tiny Lake Arthur blessed the suddenly special bit of dough.

Word of the event spread.

Neighbors built a glass-topped altar for the Rubio's living room. Beneath the glass was a palm-sized scrap of tortilla bearing the vague profile of a bearded man, set off by a spray of lavender and white plastic flowers, and a wad of cotton simulating a cloud.

Accounts of the miracle started to appear in newspapers. Pilgrims trekked to Lake Arthur from California and Mexico. A woman doing penance crawled a mile down the dirt road to the Rubio home. People would leave snapshots of afflicted relatives pinned on the Rubios' living room wall, along with metal emblems—milagros—depicting body parts in need of healing.

There were those who claimed the tortilla had cured them. A paraplegic rose from her wheelchair, Mrs. Rubio told me. Her own husband, Eduardo, a farm worker, quit drinking. At the age of 42, she bore a healthy daughter.

Thousands of the faithful and the curious flocked to the village. I was in the latter camp, number 10,191.

I telephoned the family the other morning to find out what had become of them and the tortilla.

It's no longer in their living room. Four years ago, they constructed a wooden shrine in their yard. The sunshine has faded the face a bit, but that hasn't discouraged either the Rubios or the wayfarers who come to gaze upon it.

"Every day, two or three people stop by," said Teresa Rubio, a daughter-in-law who lives nearby. "More around Thanksgiving and Christmas."

She said a few neighbors are jealous. They bellyache about strangers in town. One woman still claims Mrs. Rubio seared on the image of Jesus with a hot medallion.

But Teresa, and the Rubios, and the Rubios' six children, and who knows how many of the faithful, are undaunted.

"I believe in the tortilla," Teresa said. "It helps a lot of people."

HOLY CIRCUMCISION STILL ATTRACTS:
The unsigned letter writer's version of the column.

The only Virgin in Israel disappeared long ago but the holy circumcision hangs on. And who's to say which is more miraculous?

I didn't make it over to Goldberg Avenue to see the Virgin on the bank window. I'd hoped she'd be there longer. But with the crowds in their sanbenitos tying up traffic, the mysterious shooting of a few Palestinians and the glass man asking a million dollars for it, she wasn't.

I did view the holy circumcision—twice. Ten years ago I went to a porno store in New York in order to write a newspaper article about the circumcision. A month later I made a return trip with associates Shylok and Hormsley. The story, it seems was true.

On or about June 5, 1967, the face of Alfred E. Neumann [*sic*] appeared in the stretch marks of a circumcision being brass plated by Yehudi Rubin in Phallus, Syria. Weeping, Rubin called his banker to bear witness to the event, and interrupted his wife Golda from her coin-counting.

The rabbi in tiny Phallus blessed the suddenly special brass circumcision. Neighbors built a U.S.-built plastic alter [*sic*] for the Rubins living room. Beneath the plastic was a pearl-sized image of a freckle-faced, grinning man on the stretched tissue. It was set off by a spray of green and gold plastic flowers, and a golden dome simulating a bank.

Accounts of the miracle started to appear in newspapers. Pilgrims trekked to Phallus from New York and Jerusalem. A woman doing penance drove herself a mile down the highway to the Rubin home. People would leave snapshots of Boeske and Milkin on the Rubins' living room wall, along with chunks of the wailing wall—miracles—depicting sub-humans in need of camp.

There were those who claimed the circumcision had cured them. A newspaper writer discovered he could really spell, Mr. Rubin told me. His wife, a prostitute, became a protestant. At the age of 72 he became honest.

Thousands of the faithful merchants and those seeking to become human flocked to the village. I was in the latter camp, KIK0191, and I was given a striped uniform.

I telephoned the family the other day to find out what became of them and the circumcision. It's no longer in the living room. Four years ago, they constructed a gold and silver temple in Golan Heights. The sunshine has increased the grin and it has only served to discourage the neighboring people who might like to gaze upon it.

Every day, two or three people come by, said Sara Rubin, a daughter-in-law who lives nearby. More around Hanukkah than Thanksgiving. She said a few of the neighbors are jealous. They complain of strangers in town. One woman claims Mr. Rubin seared on the image of Neumann with a hot coin.

But Sara and the Rubins and the Rubins' two children, and who knows how many of the coin counters, are undaunted. "I believe in the circumcision," Sara said. "It screws a lot of people."

DARN THEM FREELOADERS:
It is hard to imagine so many garden-variety racists, and

their thoughtless words. Here are three short, illustrative postcard letters. While they seemed to be written by the same person, only one was signed.

This is in regard to the Weirdo that shot at the White-house [*sic*]. He has a Hispanic (Francisco Duran) name. It figures! No wonder! I have noted that the majority of crimes that are being committed involve Hispanics and most of those are "Greasers" (Mexicans)...Illegals!

Now they are causing all these protests against Prop 187 and committing vandalism. They are Stupid! They don't realize more voters will vote for 187 just because of their stupidity!

Finally, that Prop 187 is not racist! It applies to anyone who is an illegal alien! It just happens to be that 99.99 per-cent of them are greasers!

Darn them freeloaders.

GREASER-LOVIN' NEWSPAPER:

This is certainly not going to be published in your paper, is it? You seem to give top priority to stories about those "persona non grata."

I say good riddance to that Stupid Brat who burned himself to death playing with matches and gasoline! Nine years old! Those stupid parents are even more so! The Brat should have been warned about such idiotic activity! Brother!

Then about those two others who were killed by the speeding drunk! Just what were they doing out at 1:40 a.m.? Up to no good I'll bet! Most likely they were illegals involved in drugs!

This is one instance where I would say a drunken driver should be given a generous reward and a medal for ridding us of some flotsam and jetsam from Greaserland! To heck with them all! They come up here and breed like flies to produce more alleged U.S. citizens!

TO HECK WITH CINCO DE MAYO:

To all the filthy greasers: To heck with Cinco de Mayo! If you love your stinking Mexico so much, why did you ever leave? This is directed exclusively to you darn illegals! You law-breaking criminals!

I am not being racist! Anyone from anywhere who enters the U.S. without permission is included! That means Europe! My parents came from Sweden and did so legally!

I know you won't publish this, so you do not need my name.

BLEEDING-HEART LIBERALS:

A free-lance automotive specialty columnist wrote a column in which, thinking he was funny, used language offensive to a particular nationality. A follow-up column from the editor explained that the attempt at humor wasn't appreciated, and it was the genesis for forming a diversity/sensitivity task force at the newspaper. Included was mention of the intent to actively recruit minorities so the newspaper could better reflect the communities it served, and hopefully make fewer insensitive remarks in print. The letter writer returned a copy of the column with the following hand-written comments: "The press is liberal...I nominate you for wimp of the week...you have no courage...What do you have against whites?" The full letter follows:

Once again, the guilty feeling and bleeding heart liberals of your newspaper have destroyed the employment hopes of white males. According to your editor, your newspaper will no longer be looking for qualified individuals when staffing a position, but instead will be looking at their skin color, gender or both.

The editor states that the new hiring guidelines include "for every job, there must be three finalists, and at least one must be a minority. In addition, at least one in three management finalists must be a woman. The intent is to increase the number of minorities and women on staff to better reflect the communities we serve."

Excuse me, that statement tells me my husband can no longer be considered for any management position at your newspaper, no matter how well he is qualified for the job. He may be the token white male finalist but he has no chance of landing any position.

Is this any different from a person being shut out of a job because they are a minority and/or woman? Any employer who practices the opposite of this policy will be branded a racist and/or sexist.

If the editor believes this policy will achieve diversity instead of division, why doesn't he immediately resign, allowing a minority woman who can "better reflect the communities the newspaper serves" to step in?

When every individual is judged not by the color of his or her skin or by what they have or have not between their legs, but only by their own qualifications and merits, then and only then can this society achieve true diversity.

GET THE MESSAGE:

Embracing diversity as the nation continues to become a more multicultural society has been difficult for far too many newspaper readers.

I've subscribed to your newspaper for 50 years and seen so many changes, but one thing I can't get used to is the preponderance of pictures of other than Caucasians every time I pick up the paper lately. I know we are becoming a multi-cultural society of people mostly who don't care to learn English or integrate into society, but our area is still predominantly Caucasians. I wish it were reflected in the newspaper. I'm sure you don't select the pictures yourself but wish the message would get to the right person.

VIDA VISTA!

Vida Vista was a newspaper magazine supplement, which billed itself as "the magazine for all Hispanics." At the time it was published it wasn't easily zoned to the targeted audience. All subscribers received the inserted magazine. A reader returned the following message, scrawled on the cover of a young child with his grandfather (a family photo contest winner):

Refrain from trying to make this country into Mexico!

RED-NECK ATTITUDES:

Not all letters attack with the same racist force. The following two letters, written by the same author, claimed Caucasians were always given preference in stories, often to the extent that stories about "whites" and crime were being excluded.

May 13: Once again, the racist attitude of your newspaper becomes evident with your dual nature of reporting. Your newspaper reported on its front page the status of the case of those two Mexican businessmen guilty of cheating the government on contracts to the tune of $65,000 (one was a man by the name of Ortega). Now, here is a story with the amounts significantly greater, totally absent from your newspaper, and gee, they happen to be white guys. Why should anyone be surprised? Your interpretation of a free press applies only if the news is dirty, if it involves

Mexicans and if it helps to solidify the red-neck attitude that is so pervasive in society.

August 5: Since this news story [a newspaper article was clipped from another publication and attached] has not appeared in your newspaper, one can conclude that:

(1) your reporters have fallen asleep at the typewriters or word processors again, or

(2) it's more likely that because this woman is white, you and your staff have concluded she is really incapable of crime and you are deliberately withholding a news item by censoring news because a crime has apparently been committed by someone other than a Mexican or Black, in which case you would most likely run a front-page story with photo.

The blatant bias your paper continuously exhibits in the selection of news items is shallow and disgraceful, but obvious and understandable when one is aware of the history and the philosophy of your editors and white staff. Where is the objectivity and honesty of journalism? The first amendment sure takes a beating from scum bags who use their position to denigrate the unfortunate who are not white, and protect those who are.

IMMIGRANTS AND IDIOTS:

A statewide proposition concerning immigration stirred

debate across the state. Among other things, the proposition bordered on elimination of health and education benefits to illegal aliens. Students in many parts of the state protested and marched before the election to show their anger over what they believed to be racist language in the ballot measure. The proposition passed easily, but was challenged in court and ruled illegal as an appeals court judge said immigration is a federal matter, rather than a states issue. The following letter was written three days before the election:

Thank you for reporting on those two wonderful American women who held outdoor church services for homeless Americans. That's what we like to read.

But we cannot stand the almost daily blather by your Mexican reporter any longer, mostly on the front pages, reporting the rock-throwing, illegal vandals marching with the many Mexican flags. Why don't they go back to Mexico and go to school there?

Your paper is so pro-illegal. Do illegals read your paper? Well, we do, but we had just about enough of your one-sided stand and can always subscribe to another newspaper. Why don't your staff writers ever interview white Americans and write articles against these illegals who abuse our system?

Your paper reported that the county has 95,000 agricultural workers. It needs only 30,000. But we don't need even one more illegal worker, nor the years and years of invasion of the illegal, immoral Latinas who make babies like rabbits and collect billions of dollars on them. Nor do we need the millions of illegal welfare and social security cheaters collecting billions on multiple fake documents.

Your beloved Hispanic columnist looks like a criminal with his big black beard and piercing eyes, as do your other Latino male writers.

Whatever happened to the nice columns? Why is there suddenly almost no mention about Haiti, Cuba or Rwanda? We want to know.

Bravo to good Americans who dare to write letters against the invasion of illegals. We are afraid illegals would do us harm, so this is for your eyes only. Thanks for reading our letter.

P.S. Illegals still get free emergency health care. Illegals demand everything free and we dumb-balls have to pay!

WORTHWHILE NEWS:

The following letter was in response to an opinion article written by Dr. Peter Gott, a syndicated columnist:

As usual, your focus of news is crap! This Jew punk should have his privates and tongue cut out—that would be worthwhile news.

Get your head out of your you know what and feature someone worthwhile!

RODNEY KING BEATINGS:

It wasn't bad enough that Rodney King was severely

beaten by police. People continued to beat on him verbally, even after the videotape was put away. A story was published four-and-a-half years after the beating, updating King's life. Two communications followed within a couple of days, which may have come from the same author. The first was scribbled on the cut-out article, and the second was on a lined sheet of white paper.

<u>Number One:</u> Why don't you and your sob sister (the reporter who wrote the story) take this worthless ex-con and shove him. You treat him like the second coming of Christ. The cops should have shot his worthless self and one more story about him will be the last for my subscription. Is your reporter sexually involved with another reporter? They both write the same crap.

<u>Number Two:</u> Why doesn't your paper print the truth: An ex-con was hired by your "second coming of Christ" ex-con King with taxpayer's money to kill a cop. The blacks play you and your paper like a yoyo!

RACISM KNOWS NO AGE:
Adults aren't the only racists. The following letter was signed by a high school student.

I am writing in response to the article about fliers found on the high school campus.

I am a student who believes races should not be mixed. One thing I do not understand is why are the Latinos being targeted in these fliers? If someone is to be blamed it should be the white girls. They are the ones who are out there looking for Latinos and Blacks. It's not the Latinos or Blacks fault white girls don't want white men, and this is true because you mostly see white girls with Latinos or Blacks. You hardly see Mexicans or Black girls with white men.

So to all you who are planning to target other races first you should look at your white daughters and raise them right.

RACISM KNOWS NO ETHNICITY:

The following letter was apparently sent by a Latino reader.

I'm writing to you because I am very depressed to see that your newspaper seems to show an obvious favoritism to the Blacks.

In case you don't know it, we Latinos outnumber the Blacks 4-to-1 in the community, yet your press continues to display a very bias depicting Blacks in a favorable position. It seems to me the only time we Chicanos get some print is when we do something wrong.

I'm not speaking for the newly arrived Latin. Americans of Mexican descent buy your paper and we deserve more recognition and more positive input in the paper.

BLAST THE HECK OUT OF JERKS:

Readers can sometimes "read something into" a story that isn't there. One can only suppose this was the case for this person(s), in the following two letters, as they didn't provide specifics.

<u>Number One:</u> Here are glaring examples of your treatment of a news item when it involves white people. Your paper did not even mention three stories, unlike the crucifixion of the Mexican man in El Rio about five to six weeks ago who was accused of cheating tenants. You ran his [large] picture and made broad sweeps of accusations only because it suits your purpose. When you show Mexicans in a bad situation, it sells your darn paper to other bigots who believe as your news writers do. It gets darn tiresome and one sympathizes with those guys who go out and buy rifles, guns, etc., then blast the heck out of jerks who intentionally keep this kind of dissimilar treatment of events in the "news."

<u>Number Two:</u> There is no question you have a bunch of racist fools working at your newspaper, but to have such blatant evidence over and over again gets pretty depressing. Apparently it is acceptable for you to approve a story and accompanying photo of a Mexican lady and son, but it is not acceptable to run a front-page story with photos of two other stories, even though the two white people in the stories had crimes of a more serious nature. Of course your partners (sheriffs) are known for their Texas Ranger mentality.

LACK OF PATRIOTISM:
Some racists get directly to the point.

Don't see one line in your "biased" newspaper about the Japs bombing Pearl Harbor! Guess you weren't a serviceman.

Chapter Seven

O. J. and Other "Stars"

There have been some serious questions about celebrity murder and violence over the years. The most serious ones—and tragic ones—concerning the brutal deaths of Nicole Simpson and Ron Goldman.

Much of America believes it was O. J. He was, however, found "not guilty."

A less serious question, but one that gripped much of the nation, was "Who shot J. R.?"

It was 1981 and on the Dallas primetime television soap opera the man everyone loved to hate was shot.

He had pissed off or double-crossed just about everyone he knew.

Was it Bobby? Pamela? Cliff Barnes? Sue Ellen?

Naw. America had to wait until the next season, but it finally learned it was his sister-in-law, Kristen.

Several years later [a newspaper editor] was in his office

one day when the phone rang as deadline approached. Newspaper editors aren't usually very busy [a bad joke], but he waited until the fourth ring to pick up the receiver, just for effect.

"Hello, this is Larry Hagman," the man on the other end of the line drawled.

"J. R. Ewing?" the editor asked.

"In the flesh," Hagman said.

"I'm sorry, Mr. Hagman, for calling you J. R., it's just that you made such an impact on America in Dallas.

"That's OK, buddy, I get that a lot. Listen, I was wondering if you'd like to come up to the ranch for lunch."

OK, what's up, the editor thought. Why in the world would a famous "star" call a not-so-famous newspaper editor? He clearly wanted something.

"Ah, sure, why not," the editor said. "Can you give me an idea what you want to talk about?"

"I got an idea for a story," J. R. (Hagman) said, vaguely.

A date was set in about a week.

In a coat and tie, the editor was overdressed when he got out of his car and was greeted by Hagman at his multimillion-dollar ranch.

J. R. was wearing some sort of Asian-themed not-tucked-in shirt, shorts, and sandals.

The two went inside and the editor was introduced to J. R.'s wife, and his PR guy, who seemed much more arrogant than the TV star, and certainly more bored.

The editor, then a smoker, decided not to light up after learning that Hagman was a rabid antismoking champion. J. R., however, had a bourbon and branch, and offered his guest the same.

"No thanks," the editor said. "I have to drive back to work after lunch."

There was a clear agenda as they sat down for lunch.

The editor got back to the office. He felt used. Larry Hagman really wasn't his new best friend. What a pity.

Hagman, did, however, keep in touch after the editor wrote a column, even signing a videotape for the editor's sister who had long thought J. R. was something special. And, he even attended as a special guest of the editor—to attract participants—at a fund-raising auction.

Now they were both used.

A FINAL WORD FROM J. R.:

Stars aren't always too concerned with details, like the accuracy of a name. Hagman addressed the following letter to Mr. Irving (not the editor's name). Also, notice the lower-case "girls" and uppercase "boys" below. An accidental slip? Or does it say something about a man who, according to the editor's wife, was overly friendly.

Just a note to thank you for inviting me to the Boys & girls [sic] Club. It was a unique opportunity for me to meet with the movers and shakers in the town and county.

We'll see if we can spring you for lunch or dinner in Heaven [his ranch] when I get back from fishing in Oregon.

By the way, I just wanted to let you know that Mr. Barham, the Under Secretary of Commerce, will be listening to our complaints at Matilla Jr. High on June 20 at 7 p.m. This is the most important person from the government we've gotten in regard to our cause and should be crucial in deciding whether to take the tower down or not.

O. J., TWENTY-FOUR HOURS A DAY:

Life was crazy in Los Angeles during the O. J. Simpson case. The media frenzy was 24-7. Most area newspapers—and many others throughout the nation—had reporters and photographers covering every wheeze and sneeze. Live trial coverage was televised into homes and offices every day. Talk shows throughout the evening and weekend wouldn't let the topic die. No one seemed to be able to get enough O. J. Readers were no different. The following two letters, sent from someone self-named "White Rose," represented the emotionalism of the time. The second letter referenced the editor as "Grand Dragon."

I was kindling my fireplace when I suddenly remembered why I didn't cancel my subscription to the newspaper. Though useless for news, it burned well. Then by chance I came across your paper's claim that the glove that didn't fit Simpson was drenched in blood. In fact, the prosecution's glove expert admitted the amount of blood found on the glove, about three milliliters, would have "absolutely no effect" on the glove in regards to shrinkage. Are we watching the same trial, you malicious little doofi?

It's your duty to report the news, not fabricate it.

If the glove was drenched in blood, why is it that the glove had the blood drop circled in silver ink so it could be seen? Is your reporter watching the same trial, or sitting outside the courthouse with the pigeons; watching tabloid crap like Hard Copy as she earnestly takes notes?

You and your reporter—pah! Your motives are as transparent as they are disgusting. It's not the truth that matters to you, nor justice. Nor is it the freedom of a possibly innocent man. It has become apparent you want Simpson to be guilty for the basest of reasons—not necessarily because you truly believe he killed Ron and Nicole. As I watch your little rag twist the truth, I realize it is because you have the shameless depravity to want to believe he's guilty. In other words, it's not the strength of your convictions that compels you to take this stand, but the fear of losing face. As journalists this makes you useless. As human beings this shall condemn you, now and especially when Simpson is redeemed. So I saved your paper for that day, and then I'm going to circulate it nationally.

After all, I'm sure you two saps would appreciate the free publicity.

FACING THE TRUE BIGOTS:
Your newspaper is such a joke. Are you upset about the verdict? Good. I'm giggling my bottom off with your every whine and temper tantrum. It's been months since I demanded you cancel my subscription after you destroyed the respectable legacy of your past editor, but your news drop-

pings never fail to find their way to my porch like I have any intention of paying you for your rabid, dribbling froth in print. If you all weren't such a joke, I suppose I would be offended, but then I remember your circulation numbers.

Ironically, the lice colonies in your beard, and the starving earwigs in your head, desperately searching for a brain like a cranial Donner Party, shall forever amount to the most respectable part of that gangrenous pit of lies resting on your shoulders. Yet you still insist upon your right to judgment of intellectual superiors. And I can only giggle like a little girl at your pedantic imbecility.

So here's some more evidence of your own inability to face your bigotry—a letter you published today from some hysterical, racist dimwit that proves it is nothing more than a reflection of the anti-black sentiments at your paper. So she wants a boycott of Simpson and anything and anyone associated with him. Fine. But just remember that just by opening the paper we know who your advertisers are. We know exactly how to strike and where to strike without bringing you free publicity from racist sympathizers in the media.

That's if you're deemed a threat to anyone other than yourselves. But like I said—you're a joke. Regardless, we may decide to make a lesson of you useless amateurs.

To quote from your humble reader today, some hypocritical doofus: "But they are not my peers…Obviously, this jury's intelligence quotient is severely diminished. Yes, we need to evaluate the jury system."

We checked around and guess what? She's white. And she's calling the mostly Black jury stupid without even knowing who they are. That's racism! Without revealing her own I.Q. or knowing that of anyone in the jury, this biped pig in heels assumes her I.Q. is above that of anyone in the jury because they're Black and therefore biased—so much she wants to change the jury system. Now who's the stupid idiot? Who's the bigot? Both are appellations fitting to the publisher as well, because by printing such garbage they present it as acceptable debate.

Face the facts. If you want to point out the most despicable bigots in Southern California, you'll have to start by looking in the mirror. But that would imply sanity, and even as far away as here I can hear your dogs and chickens laugh whenever they see you pick up your pen and start writing; still suffering the cruel delusion you are a newspaperman.

MORE O. J., PLEASE:

After the criminal trial, the media reported O. J. sightings. He was caught one day playing golf, and a story and photos were published.

We are long-term subscribers to your newspaper and have generally been pleased by the coverage of local events and issues you have provided. We were absolutely disgusted, however, by your recent front-page coverage of O. J. Simpson playing a round of golf at Brookside Golf Course.

Is this news? Who cares? Is this person newsworthy in your estimation?

Featuring two large color pictures including that of the trailer-trash shaking hands with him through the fence was obscene. Do you have no standards? What can your reporters have been thinking? In our estimation, the only difference between O. J. Simpson and Jeffrey Dahmer is in the number killed and that O. J. wasn't hungry that night because he had just gone to the Jack in the Box.

Clearly, one or more of your reporters were buzzing around him like sycophants awaiting his every utterance so we could delight in his observations about how mean Chris Darden [prosecuting attorney] and Gil Garcetti [district attorney] are. How self-serving can you get? And you help him disseminate his 100 percent worthless opinion! This is unspeakably outrageous! Maybe (and I do mean <u>maybe</u>) five words on page 12 to inform those illogical or prejudiced minds who tout his innocence that their hero was playing golf would have been sufficient.

We wish to cancel our subscription immediately and request a refund of any balance remaining. We shall not again subscribe to your newspaper until you develop at least some rudimentary concept of journalistic ethics and your reporters learn there are some "stories" that do not deserve to see daylight.

Chapter Eight

Crazy or Mad as Hell

Death threats. Most reporters and editors don't receive them. Nor do most experience as much harassment as did crusading editor Ken Fortenberry, highlighted in chapter four. Some, however, are, on occasion, harassed or threatened by community members, newspaper readers, newspaper staff members, and even newspaper group executives and/or owners. As one tale goes, a reporter once threw a chair through an editor's office plate-glass window, during a disciplinary session. Another stood on, and peed on, his boss's desk immediately after being fired. But sometimes the harassment comes from non-newspaper types.

BASKETBALL HAS BEEN VERY GOOD TO ME:
Some years ago, a twenty-five-year-old sports reporter

loaded up his dirty yellow Ford Pinto and drove from metropolitan environs to the Big Sky of Montana. He traveled for a new job.

When he saw his first big city, Butte, he wondered what he had done. How could anyone give up smoggy and crowded Los Angeles for the mine-collapsing hills and ugly terrain of Butte? It really didn't matter that it was the home of Evil Knieval.

But traveling further north to Great Falls, he saw some hope in the wheat fields and Native American buffalo jumps.

Still, he never guessed once he settled into this new life he would be threatened.

It was a time when there was a "celebrity factor" to being a reporter, something that isn't nearly as evident today.

Reporters, then, had some prestige. Two or three times a week he would have coffee in his neighbor's kitchen, their refrigerator plastered with articles he had written, held up by tacky little magnets. The older couple was, in a way, adoptive parents. But even in those less violent days, there were some folks that weren't real nice.

He found that out one evening during the halftime of a tournament high school basketball game. Taking a break, he went to the refreshment stand and got a Coke. Returning a few minutes later, there was a folded-over piece of paper on the table where he had been taking notes and keeping statistics.

It was the most bizarre sports-related thing that had happened to him, and there had already been two almost stranger-than-fiction experiences for the city guy from Los Angeles.

First, covering a track meet shortly after this arrival to Big Sky Country, the reporter couldn't believe his eyes when a state pole vault champion contender prepared for a run at the bar. Before beginning his assault, he pulled a can of snuff from his back pocket for just a little chew, a pinch between his teeth and gums.

Then, during girls' basketball season, the reporter listened in a smoky, dingy, crowded bar to two well-off, drunken farmers betting $6,000 on a first-round Class B basketball game between area rivals.

But when he opened the note that night after getting a Coke, he couldn't believe what he read: "We didn't like what you wrote. You better watch your back because we're going to kill you. You never should have said what you did about Johnny Jones [not his real name]."

Now, the reporter didn't want to die over a sixteen-year-old high school athlete, but, at the time, it appeared he might.

Apparently his sin was one worthy of death.

Here's a recreation of his story lead [not the real teams]:

The Shelby boys' basketball team won't be going to the state tournament next week in Great Falls. It comes as a major surprise as the Mustangs were the No. 1 team throughout the regular season.

Tournaments, however, have a way of including upsets. That's what happened to Shelby as it was beat 70-69 Friday night by the Browning Indians. Still, the Mustangs could have made it to the championship tournament if guard John

Jones had been a better free-throw shooter.

Jones, a senior, missed 10 of 12 free throws during the game, including two with one second remaining. If Jones had made both of the final two foul shots the Mustangs would have led 71-70 with virtually no time left for the Indians to come back.

The reporter never completely understood what he said that prompted such hate.

"I didn't say John Jones was a 'bugger-eating moron,'" the reporter said, "even though he probably was."

The threat, never acted upon, caused the reporter to be a bit more careful, if not in his writing, certainly in late-night walks to his car after work, especially since he had recently found a homeless person sleeping in his back seat, warming himself from the bitter cold.

He also learned an interesting lesson: People in Montana take sports seriously. A California native, the reporter had a more laid-back attitude, as did Golden-state sports fans.

There were never any suspects and it was all forgotten at some point, but not before a police report was filed and he was interviewed on two of the three network-affiliated local television news shows. In those interviews he was asked why he was such an aggressive reporter, if he thought it was right to say bad things about John Jones—and if he was afraid he'd be killed.

It's hard to understand what prompts such hate in some readers and letter writers.

Crazy or Mad as Hell

ME AND MY MOM:
Some counseling clearly could have helped this anonymous letter writer.

It is sad to say, but it must be said. Everything and everyone is bad, including my mom. But she is not my mom, only step; a step down in life. No more, though, for this world.

The only way this world will be a paradise, is for me not to forgive, only forget her. Everyone who knows and thinks as her must do the same.

When in pain, think about my mom. That is why I cry. She is mean. She is cruel. She is the devil. She is a fool. She is hate. She is not No. 1. Not to me.

She's been the worst of everyone. So whenever a thought comes in your mind, always understand it is hers, not yours or mine.

Give it back to her, no one else. Think of it as a gift she earned. Not in a bad way, only in a way she wants. A world of chaos, a world of pain is all she wants. She's insane.

She is the reason for treason, taxes. You have to stop her. Think no more of numbers, they only make you hate as her. The sin within is her and only her. I will never forgive, only try to forget her. But I won't be able to until there's no more pain, no more bad, only good in the world. Please everyone help to be rid of her. Never forget her, never blame anyone but her. She did it all; the cause of all insanity and all pain.

THE FIRE OF HADES:
Editors sometimes don't even know what they've done to upset readers. Letters often fail to provide context. Such was the case in the following letter.

Tell Mr. Editor I finally found a group who will help me and your newspaper is in real hot water—boiling water. Fact is Mr. Editor is in the fire of hades! How 'bout that?

NO UNDERPANTS:
A newspaper columnist, critiquing a tour-guide pamphlet, wrote: "They may think their tour guides are hot stuff in France (where I hear they wear no underpants)." Later, the columnist wrote about "snooty French tourists, who as I said, are probably not wearing underpants." Cheap, sophomoric laughs? Yes. But was it offensive enough to warrant a reader to submit a more than 200-word letter to the editor?

Recently, I was reading an article by your columnist and I was disgusted and still am, with her attitude of tourists, particularly French tourists.

I found her article offensive and stereotypical. Naturally, it is a free country and there is such a thing as freedom of press, BUT when it gives off negative vibes like that, it is uncalled for.

We are teaching our kids to be open-minded, non-prejudicial and to understand there should be no boundaries between people. People still seem to be living in the stone age or the '50s and '60s.

I don't really want to state the content because it would just add fuel to her comments. It doesn't matter which nationality she described, it could be French, German, or whatever, even Black, Asian, and so on.

As a matter of fact, I coordinated a program over the summer for foreign exchange students who in fact were from France. I found them to be warm, conservative and had high morals. Kids are kids. Teens are going through those growing stages. And adults, like your columnist, well, I don't know.

I am involved in my kids school and don't see those kinds of attitudes being TAUGHT in the classrooms. People must pick it up from somewhere, possibly from prejudicial articles or people.

In the future, I hope articles will be printed that are free from prejudice and news that presents the positive sides, like students who ACHIEVE rather than graffiti and vandalism. Why add fuel to the fire?

A Concerned Parent,

POMPOUS IDIOT:

A columnist wrote an opinion piece about a mother who shot and killed a man accused of molesting her child. The columnist used the analogy of a mother bear protecting her cubs. A reader took exception with the columnist's sensitivity, and a scathing letter was published. But that wasn't good enough for the following anonymous letter in response to the published letter.

Amen! Your columnist is a pompous idiot; an unreasoning, un-researched babbling demagogue. The editors should have said, "yes, we have an editorial on these serious matters, but you are unqualified to write it."

We call her old one shot; 10 minutes at the word processor with no rewrites.

Dump this moron before she embarrasses you further. And show a current picture in the meantime; she must have gained 50 pounds.

IN-YOUR-FACE:

Many newspaper editors will try to correspond with letter writers who request a response. Some will also respond if they believe a simple point of clarification needs to be made. Such was the case below, when a letter writer responded to an editor's earlier letter that pointed out in a pleasant way that the writer was "ill-informed" concerning a certain fact.

If I'm ill-informed, as you suggest (in your letter), it's the fault of your lousy liberal paper. You're the one who informs me. You must not be doing a very good job.

I'm afraid you're the one who's ill-informed. We've seen what's happened to your newspaper in recent years, from the crazy feminine format to the major metropolitan philosophy.

BASTARDIZATIONS:

A long history of anger sets off some writers. Or, it could be a personal vendetta or just a frustration with the world or society in general. While some may explain what has angered them, there usually is much more in the letter than the specified complaint. When readers go over the edge, they often times cancel their subscriptions—after giving the editor an earful.

There is no shortage of excellent newsprint in the area, but your newspaper remains one of the worst of its kind—content, editorial policy, substance and timely news. It is no secret the newspaper and its illegitimate parent [corporate owner], in their anti-firearm policy, are going to go Chapter 11, along with your agenda.

I find the editing and re-writing of my letters to the editor a bastardization of the original, unacceptable and intellectually dishonest as well.

When you called for suggestions to improve this rag, we took you at your word. Your word isn't good, and your staff members are liars for hire!

You had three opportunities to straighten out your crass act, and with this third strike you're out! Just note, I shall never forget those who pay your bills.

Take me off your subscriber list immediately, and

NEVER, EVER think of having anyone call my home to re-subscribe.

BOILING HOT!

Almost anything can fuel the fires. The following letter was in response to a minor change in stock quotations.

I am livid with rage at what you've done to the financial pages! Whose brilliant idea was that? Because of it, a few of my friends and I have dropped your paper.

What are you planning on filling you're newly found space with? The likes of one of your writing hacks who should be writing for a high school yearbook?

Some of our stocks are not even listed! This was the main reason I bought your provincial newspaper.

If you do not list complete financial coverage you'll lose a lot more customers! I never heard of such a system!

I am boiling! Cancel my subscription.

NOT MAD, JUST A BIT OFF CENTER:

It's easier to read a letter from someone who is mentally troubled, rather than "mad as hell." But it is also more depressing, especially, for some reason, when the person appears extremely intelligent. It's also easy to have feelings of sorrow for those who deal with demons and allusions. The following letter included six classified ads in which the author was seeking free publication. The primary purpose was to seek money.

My hope is that you may receive what I am about to share with you with all grace, dignity and sobriety, that you may stand in the unexpected, which throughout all our entire lives was suspected. I feel confident having chosen the profession you find yourself in, you are of conscious persuasion that there are those things, seemingly stranger than fiction! Of one such I commence to relate.

Several years ago I found myself in the beginning development of an apostleship appointment, having received initiation in ambassadorship into a group labeled the "reserve corps of destiny," whereby I had revealed the potential of the arena I had elected to participate in, having been a candidate for some years. Quite frankly, I never dreamed I would be the one pushing these two pens today, howbeit through the mind's eye I am well read in possibility and responsibility beginning at an early age, searching the awakening. Part of the requirement is that a man be able to work quietly without a lot of fanfare, the popular art of drawing attention to oneself. I have the liberty to work with others, but only in an atmosphere of confidential trust, as a man may be found who discovers God resident within himself, and that all is of record in love with expanding eternal values. In other words, our planet is undergoing some astronomical changes in nature as well as the understanding of men, adjusting how they view the reality and embrace of life.

My initiation was personally through one Incarnation who calls himself Christ Michael and had manifested as such since 1984. It sounds much like Big Brother! I have exercised the liberty as well as the privilege and responsibility of extensive travels overseas living and traveling with Him and among Him. And, it is seldom manifested in the physical, according to the desires and imaginations of the childish and selfish minds among men. Most of the professing "Church" alive today would crucify afresh the Son of God and man. I'm sure, in your position, you have observed a sufficiency in life to understand the things I say, and there is always recourse toward further inquiry!

This means that Christ is returned, according to promise. The question remains how shall it now proceed to unfold, according to the listening in consistency through one's own personally prepared filter in righteous trust, which of every man it is required? "Unto whom much is given, much is required." Free-will election has been parceled out to all men to test the preparation of heart.

If Christ is returned, then what questions would men have, or rather ought they to have? How may I help is the voice of sincerity and service, the duty of man to responsibility as his opportunity awaits the betterment of civilization and the hope of all men throughout the ages. Faith is an act that is required of the son who recognizes his sonship and call of His Universe Father. Man can no longer restrain the expansion of cosmic consciousness, the transfer into the next millennium, the dawning of the age of Light and Life.

There is a tide in the affairs of men which taken at the flood lads on to fortune, omitted, all the voyage of their life is bound in shallows and in miseries. On such a full sea are we now afloat, and we must take the current when it serves or lose our ventures.

My commitment in promise to you for your support in co-contribution is to keep you apprised of developments along the line of unfolding ramifications for an event of such perceived magnitude and it is actually much bigger than you ever imagined, but we prefer to keep it as low key as possible.

The hope of our children's children and beyond their progeny depends upon the generational awakening that is found as a germinating seed within the hearts of all courageous men and women commanding their life post in responsibility before God and potential service to mankind.

Would you be kind enough to pursue the enclosed ads and share with me your comments regarding those avenues which you perceive might yield the more abundant fruits? My resources of pocket are dwindling from several years of living, and traveling, serving from savings and, all Christ received upon arrival was a body and all power in Heaven and earth. As we are all participants in light and awakening together, the acknowledgement of the light within also activates the services of our brethren, the angelic and seraphic host, who are here in legions to participate in the ascension program of both men and angels. Fear not!

Thank you for your professional courtesy as well as your service in time and space to Him who gave it. In all sincerity and verity,

The Apostle

LONG LIVE FLAG DAY—AND BEARDS:
The combination of complaints sometimes makes little sense.

I am mad as heck. This is "Flag Day" and you put the best thing in your liberal paper on the back page and a big article about a graffiti artist on the front page.

Don't see much about your "Slick Willie," [Bill Clinton] but you sure blasted former presidents Reagan [Ronald] and Bush [George].

Thank goodness you got rid of that beard!

Chapter Nine

In Jesus' Name

Reporters, editors, and newspaper workers, in general, have long had reputations of not being shy when it comes to alcohol consumption. Not too many years ago, many had bottles of vodka, gin, or whiskey in the bottom drawers of their desks.

Drinking and conversation sessions are regularly held after deadline at neighborhood bars and pubs. Most towns have a "newspaper bar" nearby, frequented by workers ranging from mailroom stuffers to printers, to ad sales representatives to reporters.

Many, many stories are told. One night, an editor thought he was going to have his heart cut out by a religious sect.

It had been a long day-night at work. The editor, who had begun work at 10 A.M., made it to the bar around 10 P.M. At about 3 A.M., he literally rolled into the front room of his condominium, after five-hours of nearly nonstop drinking. His poison had been wine, of the Chablis variety.

He was a bit fried. Still, the hearty soul poured another glass of wine from the box in his refrigerator. He made a peanut butter, bologna, and cheese sandwich and sat down to watch TV.

The phone rang.

He picked up the receiver, but not before the fourth ring, so the recorder kicked in. He was hoping it might be a friend who would be interested in stopping by for some companionship. He slurred a "halloo" into the mouthpiece and then listened to a very distraught woman yelling and chanting voodoo phrases.

It went on for a couple of minutes before he hung up the phone, sweating from the final words the Haitian woman had uttered.

As she calmly stopped her chant, she clearly said the re- porter's full name and address. Then she told him she'd be right over to cut his heart out because of the relationship he was having with her sixteen-year-old daughter.

She explained she would then boil and eat his heart to cleanse her daughter.

Something was wrong. Seriously wrong.

He wasn't having an affair with a sixteen-year-old girl. Yes, he was separated from his wife, and dating a few thirty-year-old women, but certainly no sixteen-year-olds. Nor had he written anything about sixteen-year-old girls, at least as best he could remember, in his state of the moment.

He called the cops. They took a report, but wouldn't come out. Some lame excuse about prank phone calls and being too busy.

So he stayed awake the rest of the night—wide-eyed, with a baseball bat in hand—hoping he wouldn't learn more about the voodoo religion and Haitian culture.

There were no visits, nothing going bump in the night. A phone call the next morning from the police assured him his worries about death or a shotgun wedding were over. It seems he and another fine citizen shared the same name. And it seemed the Haitian mother had figured out her error shortly after the phone call.

It was unclear if a visit had been paid to the other residence.

THE *GHOST STORY CLUB* COMIC STRIP:

A new comic strip was being introduced into the newspaper. A note was included the first day it appeared: "We're featuring *Ghost Story Club*, a new comic strip for young readers, for a two-week trial period. Please take a look and tell us what you think. A ballot will be published in Sunday's *Voices* section." Before the ballot was even published, the following letter arrived, along with an article on teenage suicide, and an article on a teenage murder.

I have already voted—the enclosed stories are the harvest from a single day's news. These are examples of the cult of death being promoted in our society. You will have to answer to God for your decisions—whether you serve life or serve death.

EUGENE CHANGEY:

There probably aren't too many editors who aren't familiar with Eugene Changey of Maple Heights, Ohio. Eugene sent letters to editors across the country for years. Very few were ever published, even though some editors made reference to him, usually in a disparaging way, in personal columns. Following are six letters and "treatises" from Eugene, including a letter "dictated" by a deceased John F. Kennedy and a conversation with the former president following his death.

Number One: As Almighty GOD, I greet you:

My HOLY SPIRIT is Dictating this Holy Letter through My humble Son, Eugene/Jesus. They are ONE combined SPIRIT...Reincarnated!

My son (a BACHELOR all His life) resides with His spinster sister in Maple Heights, Ohio. She owns the house and car. The telephone is also listed in her name.

In Our fifty-odd years together, We have mailed COUNTLESS numbers of Holy Form-Letters mainly to newspaper Editors and Publishers. The responses in return have been pitifully few in proportion to the Letters sent. A majority of the replies have been from MONGRELS...who are NOT GOD-FEARING!

Upon the demise of My Son (I Am IMMORTAL and cannot die) many MONGRELS will emerge from the wood-work to help blasphemy from hypocrites in obnoxious columns in newspapers throughout the World. In times past, We have mailed MANY Form-Letters to English-speaking Countries.

With reluctance, My Holy Words will fade into the Distance, as My Dictation will end. My Holy Name is void of Form…so it is NEVER written on paper. My Son will sign His SURNAME to preserve a FAITH that will NEVER DIE!

Prayerfully yours,

P.S. Please publish the interesting Treatise (below), written by My Son, with My Assistance.

Number Two: Father, GOD, has asked that I write this Letter personally. With a meager ninth-grade education, I cannot attribute my knowledge to myself. True knowledge can only come from GOD.

The following are excerpts—with a few revisions—from Our Books: GOD'S LIGHT (1968) and RETURN TO GOD (1969) published by Carlton Press, New York, N.Y. Carlton Press is a subsidy publisher. I paid to have Our Works published.

These essays are not written by my Father and I to make a World's population Psychotic or Neurotic, on the contrary. We do it to make a World understand reality—how GOD'S Holy SPIRIT, in human flesh, has withstood the ravages of wars throughout centuries. This is how HE Exists today, in this dimension of Time and Light.

Prayer is sustenance that has kept My Father's Holy SPIRIT alive from the beginning of Recorded Time.

And now, Our excerpts from GOD'S LIGHT:

I admit I have a split-personality. Didn't Jesus have one? I don't regard this as blasphemy! The SPIRIT of GOD was in Jesus—they were two in one body, the same as today.

Jesus said: "Wretched is the body which is bound to a body. And wretched is the soul bound to these two together." Dead Sea Scrolls.

An introvert, such as I am, is more likely to suffer from schizophrenia than an extrovert. But alas, each and every human has a measure of schizophrenia, no matter how great or small!

Every living creature, that can distinguish the difference between good and evil, has a persecution complex!

Perhaps the dictionary defines a persecution complex in its own way. Here is how the Bible defines it:

No servant can serve two masters; for either he will hate the one, and love the other; or else he will hold to the one, and despise the other. Ye cannot serve God and mammon. Luke 16:13.

There are two immense forces that control our destiny and our way of thinking, a force of good and a force of evil. These two forces oppose each other. The persecution arises, when one is in derision as to which force to follow.

The main reason many people fear GOD, is because they have a persecution complex. Their fears are centered on their past sins and inferiority to GOD. They are in fear of punitive measures that may be taken against their will.

There is one consolation: perfect and true Love can cast out fear.

The following are excerpts from: RETURN TO GOD.

In my case—from solitary thinking—thoughts can be expounded through Light.

There are two sources of LIGHT. One from GOOD and one from EVIL. GOD is connected invariably with the GOOD LIGHT. The Devil is connected with the EVIL LIGHT.

Personally, I tend to strive toward that which is good, but in this form of life on Earth, this is almost a physical and mental impossibility. When one is contended with two forces, these tend to sway one from the other.

No single human thought, or action, is ever discarded. They are infinite. They are also used on Judgment Day for or against a person.

If the criminal of today, knew of his impending fate, he would not perpetrate acts of violence. It is written: Whatsoever ye sow, so shall ye reap. If they live in violence, their ultimate destruction shall be violent!

The criminal is condemned two fold: (1) His moral obligation to society. (2) His moral obligation to GOD. If he escapes the first, he cannot possibly escape the second. Consequently, he pays a higher debt. This is the ultimate price one must pay for crime.

For the criminal, my Father and I leave a legacy of fear. For the Christian, We leave a legacy of LOVE.

My Father and I bid you a fond anon.

Number Three: As Almighty GOD, I greet you:
My Son, Eugene/Jesus (they are ONE combined

SPIRIT—Reincarnated) is writing My Dictation, as the HOLY SPIRIT in His body...which is My Holy Temple.

For Christians (and other Denominations) who are unaware as to how TWO SPIRITS in ONE Body communicate, the answer is simple: My Son tries to keep His mind a total blank...free from thoughts. My Holy Voice is heard above the void. Thus He rapidly writes My very Words.

Bishop Fulton J. Sheen became a part of destiny when President Kennedy was assassinated. My Son wrote to the Bishop about the Existence of the President's Spirit in My Son's Body...an experience which proves a departed Spirit, from a defunct body, can be reincarnated into another live body, as My Son, through Light and time. Thus a departed Spirit is free to come and go through Light, or remain stationary throughout the life of a being, human or animal, according to My Whim.

The enclosed Treatise was mailed to his Holiness Pope John Paul II. He has been on Our mailing-list over three decades.

Please do humanity a favor and publish these Letters of Faith and Love to Me...your CREATOR.

With Love and Devotion, My Dictation through My Son will cease, as He will lay His pencil down and proceed to type this Holy Letter. My Holy Name is void of Form, so it is never written on paper. My humble Son, Eugene/Jesus, will sign His SURNAME to convey Our Love to you

Prayerfully yours,

Number Four: November 25, 1963
Most Rev. Fulton J. Sheen
366 Fifth Avenue
New York, N.Y.

Dear Reverence:

I thought of a great many persons to whom I should send this letter. I thought of Our new President, Lyndon B. Johnson. I thought of Mrs. Kennedy, but perhaps in her time of grief, this letter would not have been appropriate.

Now I turn to you, dear Reverence. This is a lonely world and one must turn to another for kind understanding. You, my dearest Reverence Sheen, are very dear to my Father's Heart.

Friday, as my Father and I worked at Our job, We heard the tragic, unbelievable news of President Kennedy's death. My Father sadly exclaimed: "We have been set back one hundred years!"

Saturday, I was fully aware of the President's existence with Us, i.e. his spirit. This day, he seemed in the best of spirits—highly elated—as many times during the day that broad Kennedy grin would light my face as We talked and joked.

The President was in the best of spirits as he laughed, "When did this happen?" He referred to my existence with my Father.

Sunday was different, he seemed extremely depressed.

"When will Jackie see me, Son?" he asked sadly. (He called me "Son" because that is how my Father refers to me.)

I couldn't find words to console him, but I replied: "Someday Jackie will see you, John, and your dearest children will follow."

John often keeps calling for Jackie. My Father explains to me, she is all he turns to.

My Father says John cries quite frequently. My Father explains things to me because I take these darn tranquilizers—under doctor's prescription—and unfortunately I cannot comprehend the depths of my mind as I used to.

This Sunday, John asked three or four times to pray for Jackie. Perhaps I was a little perplexed with the frequent inquisition, but my Father each time asked me to oblige.

I went to my room, kneeled beside my bed, and John prayed for Jackie and the children. Unfortunately I can't recall his words, but he spoke with eloquence.

I've never heard of a man with such a great devotion to his wife and children.

John seemed aware of Our financial plight to have Our works published. Several times he said: "Jackie will help you, Son."

It's so embarrassing for me to relate this, as Our job is sufficient to keep Us alive.

Monday, the President seemed to be in good spirits, but he would often lapse into fits of depression. Again, my Father said, he cried frequently.

At Our job—at one time—I was filing a piece in the machine when the President asked: "Let me do that, Son!"

I obliged and the three of Us filed the piece together.

"Do you have to do this?" John asked referring to Our work.

"We don't have to," I replied. "We could starve!"

John burst out laughing as that Kennedy grin broadened my face.

This Monday, the voice of the President has been gradually fading, as he goes on to a greater glory, in a heaven beyond, to hold grace in God's Eyes.

At one point, John asked: "Can't I stay with you, Son?"

"That is up to my Father," I replied.

Given time, I believe John will conform to his surroundings in another world, patiently awaiting his beloved Jackie.

I've often talked with my dear departed mother, who once said: "Ez jo clet." This is a good life. She often seems proud of me that I hold grace in God's Eyes.

Please do not regard this letter as a personal confession, Reverence. As I mentioned earlier, I wanted to turn to others. You may show this letter to whom your heart desires.

I pray you understand Us, my loving Fulton J. Sheen. Each night before I go to bed, I pray faithfully for you.

My Father sends His Love, as We bid a fond farewell.

Prayerfully yours,

Number Five: Dictated November 22, 1983

A MESSAGE FROM THE PAST

On this, the twentieth anniversary of my demise, I, John Fitzgerald Kennedy, am dictating this letter of survival of my holy spirit through the body of our beloved Son and Savior.

Indeed I am alive in spirit, which is the legacy of our beautiful Father, Almighty God. I am proud to say a soul never dies, insomuch as it would in an earthly demise. These past few decades have rewarded me with abounding love from our Father and Savior into a realm of reality that a soul can actually live if it be the will of Justice. I, a sinner, have been granted life in another dimension of time. I was spared the agony of hell, where many unfruitful souls must languish—according to the testimony of our Father and Savior.

Time has a tale to tell of past remorseful sins—of which I have been spared the humility. This is a tranquil life as depicted by many other souls, who have been granted asylum by a forgiving Father and His beloved Son.

I do not know what the future holds, but I sum up my past fears about life after death, and serve my God and Savior with dignity. I can see and converse with a multitude of souls that have gone before me, to grant wisdom to the destitute—but proud in spirit.

I wish to thank the heavenly father and Son for their condolence in making me believe that others can and will share their abode in heaven, just as other souls travel through time and space in a never ending, abundant realm of love and understanding.

Now I must bid a fond anon, as our Son and Savior's pencil must end this letter of love and patience to others, who will eventually follow in my footsteps.

My love I extend to Jacqueline, Caroline and John. I bless the Father and Savior for keeping this light of love and understanding lit for future participants to this chapter of glory. I shower my blessings on all who have kept the faith that will never die.

With love I remain,
John Fitzgerald Kennedy

Number Six: It didn't pay to get on Eugene's bad side. Following is a letter to an editor who asked to be taken off Eugene's mailing list.

Mr. Doe:

My Son and I received your letter requesting that We take your name off Our mailing list. We will do just that...but you will NOT have the last words between Us!

We were always under the impression that a newspaper should print the news that is worthy of publication. You degrade My Son and Me of that objective. Perhaps you believe murder, rape and mayhem is all that the public want to read about?

As Almighty God, My Holy Spirit is alive and breathing in My Son's Flesh and not lost in the sky or pages of the Bible! When My Name has lost its reader-appeal, the fury and hell your putrid hyde [*sic*] will feel! Out of 1,200 editors and publishers (over the past few years) your rejection was only the third We received. We will replace your foul name with one, who perhaps, will be more worthy of Us.

Upon your demise, you will look toward your puny god for consolation, but alas, I Am the Only God you will see when you open your eyes in another Dimension of Life!

My Son and I are here to stay, 'till Death tells Us to depart and not flirt with human feelings that sway the heart! You may tear this letter up in pieces but My Biting Words will live in your memory, until your demise.

So We ring down the curtain on another idiot who believes he can live without a Real Live God. Thus ends My Dictation through My Son until the final day of Judgment. My Holy Name is Void of Form, so it is Never written on paper. My Son, Eugene/Jesus, will sign His Surname to end Our Correspondence.

Condemningly yours,
Eugene Changey

PRAYER FOR THE DAY:

Newspaper clustering and consolidation saw the merging of two nearby local daily newspapers. One, published in a conservative and aging community, featured a daily prayer on its editorial page. The other newspaper was circulated in a younger and more liberal community. The prayer, definitely "Christian" in substance, was generally nonthreatening and loved by the majority of the elderly and long-term subscribers. In the consolidation effort, the two newspapers now shared many of the same pages, including expanded editorial pages. Trying not to take anything away from readers, the daily prayer was retained as part of the shared pages. But it seemed almost as if the first shot had been fired in a Holy War. Jews, atheists, and others fired off letter after threatening letter. Here are four of the best (or worst):

Number One: Here is my suggested prayer for the day: Please send us a new editor who isn't an ethnocentric bigot, and who recognizes the responsibility to portray an unbiased viewpoint, especially with regard to other peoples' religious beliefs or non-beliefs.

Number Two: Since you are continuing pro and con votes on your daily prayer, you can add my vote to the con column.

I think your view is misguided and naive. Of course, as a member of the Christian majority, you see nothing wrong with a daily prayer to Christ and cannot understand why anyone would object. But as a Jew, I consider prayer to Jesus to be blasphemy. The First Commandment prohibits prayer to a man if he were a god. Jews and many others consider Jesus to be just a man. We don't go around telling Christians that because we don't want to cause the kind of hostility that you claim you are trying to avoid. But your little prayer is a daily insult to me, a reminder that non-Christians don't count in your paper or in this country.

You grudgingly state you will "consider" printing prayers from other religions. Obviously, you are not being even-handed in this. How about printing this:

Oh Lord, I pray for the day that people will quit worshipping Jesus as if he were a god and recognize that all men and women are equal before God?

Or how about this:

There is but one true God and Mohammed is his only true prophet.

Offensive, aren't they? But maybe for a moment you understand how offended I am by your prayers.

Also, while you report in today's paper that there is increased racism nationally, you continue to promote a single belief. This is Anti-American!

Number Three: Your paper has changed so many times in the past few years, it's hard to keep up. However, when I read of the current changes, I hoped you, Mr. Editor, would make the best change of all; eliminate the "today's prayer" which is so controversial to many readers. Alas, it was not to be! However, since you claim to be so dedicated to fairness, maybe you should print the following partial selection of Bible verses seldom mentioned in sermons.

II Kings 19:35: God sends an angel to slaughter 185,000 human beings in one night.

II Kings 2:23-24: God sends two bears out of the forest to kill 42 children.

Numbers 16:27-35: God buries alive mothers and their children and then burns up the fathers.

Numbers 31:17-18: Moses tells an army to kill all male children and all non-virgins and to keep all the virgins and girl children for themselves.

Luke 12:47-48: Jesus advises that the proper way to punish slaves is with a severe beating.

I Corinthians 11:7: A man is the image and glory of

God, but a woman is only the glory of man.

Then, hereafter, pick one of your quotes, then one of the less known and less loved ones. I won't hold my breath, though.

Number Four: I am hereby canceling my 14-year subscription to your newspaper because I cannot philosophically agree with your policy to publish Christian prayers. The notion of a daily benediction is not offensive, particularly if it is done in an egalitarian manner. That is, if all religions were equally represented, the community would benefit from greater awareness of both shared thoughts (i.e. the Golden Rule) and in unique differences. While you report in today's paper there is increased racism nationally, you continue to promote a single belief. This is Anti-American!

Rethink your policy and readdress the benefits of diversity.

THE FAR RIGHT:

Labels are easy. For instance, all reporters are liberal. But perspective does help in identifying people. The following letter was in response to dating classified ads:

Please accept our regrets. Your journalism is extremely slanted toward abortion and homosexuality! We don't appreciate your sick ads promoting porno and AIDS. You are too biased for our family.

GOOD NEWS, BAD NEWS:

Readers often complain that newspapers don't print positive news, only what is negative. That is a wrong assertion. Surveys will show newspapers publish more positive news than negative news, yet the negative is the most easily remembered:

More than 50,000 men and boys met at the Anaheim Stadium May 14–15 for the purpose to promise to obey God's Word, help their fellow men, practice high morals, build strong marriages and families and reach beyond racial and denominational barriers to demonstrate unity.

Now, I call this Good News, but I haven't read one item about it. I wonder if it had been a group of gays, feminists or gang members if the outcome would have been different. I think so.

One other thing. In 1990, there were 75 men. Now there are more than 50,000 in one of six group meetings, so they aren't going away by being ignored. It is the double standards of the media that boggle my mind.

Chapter Ten

Politically Speaking

The reporter and photographer parked an older automobile with rusting paint, three hub caps, and a dented bumper on the street in front of multimillion-dollar homes in Pacific Palisades, just up from the brilliant sea and sandy beaches of Southern California's Pacific Ocean.

They walked up a winding driveway and were met about halfway to the mansion by a long, black limousine.

It stopped and the back window slid down by the touch of an inside button.

"Hello, Charlene. Hello, John," the salt-and-pepper-haired, good-looking, well-dressed man said as he leaned his head out the window.

"Nancy's up at the house waiting for you. I'm sure you will all have a nice day."

The tinted window slid shut and the limo stretched down the driveway and onto the street.

Here today, gone today. It was the former B-picture actor, current governor of California, and future president of the United States, on his way to the Sacramento office. Ronald Reagan of Bedtime for Bonzo **fame.**

It was a surprise and shock for the reporter. Yes, he knew he'd be taking photos of California's First Lady, Nancy, but he never dreamed he'd talk with Ronnie. Well, OK, they really didn't carry on a conversation.

What was shocking was the governor would call him by his first name. Sure, the names of the reporter and photographer had been submitted in advance in the name of security, but there was a lesson to be learned.

Politicians are slick. They are almost always on stage, practicing public relations, developing relationships, cultivating acquaintances, all to be used at some point to their advantage.

Politicians often try to use the media—and the public; and society seems to grow more and more politically polarized every day.

While many readers don't seem to care much for politics, some are loyal Democrats, or Republicans, or whatever. And they are easily angered if they perceive a media bias for or against certain politicians or affiliations.

SLICK WILLIE:

You're darned if you do and darned if you don't. That saying fits newspapers when it comes to politics. Kill the messenger (or editor) is also appropriate. Newspapers are often blamed for whatever ails the reader. The following two unsigned letters, possibly from the same author, are classic examples.

Number One: I just wanted to thank all of you in the press for single-handedly getting your boy "Slick Willie" elected.

I am so excited about his priorities to improve America. Just imagine homosexuals in the military! How in the world have we survived to this point without it? And free worldwide abortions! He said he would create jobs and just think of how many more abortion doctors we will need! More time off for federal employees, boy oh boy, just what we need (and cutting a few servants in the White House). Bold moves, all! Thanks again.

Number Two: Boy are you ever on top of things! You missed the end of the recession by about a year!

Fact is you hid it from the American people in order to get your boy "Slick Willie" in.

Your cover-up of the economic conditions in this country was worse than Iran-Contra and Watergate combined.

Rush Limbaugh is going to have a ball with this. "Media found guilty in Recession-gate cover-up."

Just how stupid do you think we are?

P.S. Happy Easter.

IN MEMORY OF DICK NIXON:

It is often said there are two things friends should not talk about—religion and politics. Those subjects, however, are possibly the two most talked about subjects in letters to the editor. And, there is no shortage of strong opinion.

Kent State...Cambodia...The Wall...More than 58,000 brutally murdered in the line of duty...Spiro Agnew...Watergate...Domestic Espionage...Presidential Tax Evasion...People's Enemy Hit List...John Lennon.

My heartfelt condolences to the Nixon family on this great new American holiday...the day Satan himself died.

Maybe people and the history books have already forgotten or they just don't care anymore but the EVIL genius did more to hurt the cause of America than anyone before him. To his benefit, only Ronald Reagan and George Bush were more evil and mean-spirited.

Consider this: As a Vietnam veteran, it offends me when I hear that "King Richard" was instrumental in a quick and honorable peace. As I recall the war lasted at least 10 years, the last five of which were the bloodiest times in American history. Army grunts, Navy Swabbies and Marine Leather-necks kicked Victor Charlie in the pants, winning every single encounter with Uncle Ho's boys. Air Force B-52s from my unit blew Charlie back to the Stone-age during Operation Linebacker—in effect ending the war in 30 days. 10 years? 30 days? Sounds like a long, long war that made someone a huge profit and it surely wasn't you or I!

Consider this: American troops on American soil. As an American soldier I took an oath swearing to uphold and defend the Constitution of the United States. The Constitution guarantees freedom of speech, bans slavery, the right to assemble and the freedom to publicly protest against the government without fears of reprisal. Yet people died at Kent State and Jackson State, thousands were beaten at the conventions in Miami, Chicago and in too many cities across America. How many of you reading this lost a dad, brother, husband or friend in 'Nam? Well, my family and I did. Did you or he want to be there? None of us did! A quick end to the war? Why are thousands of families still waiting to hear of their loved ones 20 years after the fact?

Consider this: For all the power Mr. Nixon had, he feared those people who were perceived to have more. FBI, CIA & IRS files were filled with records of actors, musicians and writers because they controlled the media. Case in point—John Lennon of Beatles fame was considered dangerous because he promoted peace and an alternative way of life. More important was the fact that as a member of the most famous rock band in history, he could effectively reach millions thus creating the largest army in the world. Hence, the People's Enemy Hit List. Were you on it? Don't know? Use the Freedom of Information Act to find out.

Last but not least, consider this: Richard Milhous Nixon twice swore to uphold the Constitution, a document baptized by American blood and an ideal I hold sacred, both times showing total disregard for the sacrifices of Americans. The prime example of course is Watergate and Tricky Dick's henchmen. Enough has been said and written about this crime against America that I don't need to say any more on that subject. However, in closing I would like to paraphrase Mr. Nixon with these words: "We think that when someone dies, if we lose an election, or suffer a defeat that all is ended…this is not true. It is only a beginning."

Rest in peace if you can Mr. Nixon, because you are about to embark on a journey across the river Styx to receive your eternal reward.

A LETTER FROM I. P. FREELY:
During his eight years as president, Bill Clinton was an easy target and focus of several letter writers.

Hey! I've got a question. Your cartoonist recently listed three things which Clinton had going for him over Dole. They were CBS, NBC and ABC. He could have listed CNN, New York Times, L.A. Times, Associated Press, your newspaper and many other liberal media dispensers.

Just WHY does the media go for the liberal truth? It seems to me all people should be interested in a balanced budget, lower taxes and welfare reform. Certainly Clinton espoused these items, but he lied, he did not mean what he said. At least he hasn't delivered. He did not approach the idea of a balanced budget until the Republicans forced him.

The news media always has some critical remark when they are reporting on a conservative idea, but a great deal of enthusiasm when reporting on a liberal subject.

Perhaps they want to be overly critical on some subjects

and much less critical on others. The media gave more and continuing reporting on Dan Quales [*sic*] misspelling of potato than they did of the Chappaquadic [*sic*] escapade and resulting cover-up of Teddy Boy Kennedy. If a conservative senator was involved in such an occasion there would have been a congressional hearing of the ethics committee and the press would still be bellowing.

The media has a credibility gap. Perhaps it fails to report things which should be reported and twists and implies the stories which it reports. Using the words "on the condition of anonymity" means it is a lie or fabrication, and the writer is trying to give the impression he has information no one else has.

Much is being reported about the minimum wage and as you write, "true campaign reform." Now it is up to Gingrich & Dole to take care of these problems. Editors and reporters say they should do something about these subjects. Yes, even the politicians (liberal ones, that is). Where were the politicians and media on this subject before November 1994? They had the executive and congressional branches? Why didn't they do something then? Please advise.

Also, it would be nice to hear from you about the *Reader's Digest* article titled "The Clintons and the Union Boss." How did this one slip out? Does the news media know about this?

Hey! You could do a lot of writing answering these questions. Don't bother writing me as I know many of your readers wouldn't want to hear the answers in your liberal talk.

Yours Truly,
I. P. Freely

P.S. Regarding this "legal defense fund" for Clinton. Shouldn't he report that as income? If not, can a private citizen do the same? Also, keep Mallard Duck on the editorial page. It really adds something!

Chapter Eleven

In Your Face

The distraught woman walked in the front door of the newspaper office. She was screaming, not bloody murder, but about a bloody murder.

Her son had been shot and killed in a drive-by shooting.

She wasn't pleased the newspaper had reported the tragedy.

The clerk at the front desk didn't know what to do. She was afraid the woman would become violent.

The woman held her hand in her purse, one big enough to conceal a gun.

The newspaper editor heard the commotion and came out of his office to intercede. He rescued the young, terrified clerk, but began worrying about his own safety as the woman had yet to remove her hand from the bag, which seemed to be grasped onto something.

He got her into his office and listened to her story. She had every right to be upset. Her baby had been killed, and the story of his gangster life and death was now being told to thousands of readers; some even family, friends, and peers of the dead youngster.

How does a mother lose a son, regardless of the cause? The pain is the same.

The woman screamed, and talked, and screamed, and talked. The editor listened.

He agreed when he could. He told her time and again he was sorry for her loss. He explained why the newspaper had written a story. But he got a better story about a mom's love. She took her hand out of her purse, clutching only tissue. She wiped her eyes.

A half hour later she was as calm as a mother can be who has just lost a son. The editor walked her to the door, gave her a hug, and told her to come back or call if she wanted to talk.

Far too many readers have no problem with getting in your face. Most, however, can be disarmed face-to-face just by a journalist being a good listener. But there is certainly power in the pen, and letter writers like to exercise it.

PERSONALITY CONFLICT? YOU THINK?

The following three letters were unsigned, possibly from the same unhappy reader, attacking an editor's weekly column and policy decisions.

Number One: Dear Arrogant Jerk:

This is an update on how we personally feel about your trashy newspaper.

You always hit people below the belt when they are not looking, with your negative actions and deeds.

You print you are a God-fearing newspaperman and sneer at people to whom you feel morally superior. Yet in your paper you print entertainment for adults, escorts for hire. Isn't this a form of prostitution?

You print cartoons on various people whom you wish to bring down to your level, through fear and anger, whatever suits your purpose. You misuse the press to manipulate and insinuate, instead of to inform and educate.

What's the matter? No guts to stand up for your principles, or no principles to stand up for?

Precisely which church did you learn these values in? Most of us follow the God of love. Clearly you follow the God of hate and malicious mischief. What kind of example are you setting for the impressionable youth of this community?

Number Two: Dear Crybaby:

I don't share your disappointment over the recent article you published on Mr. and Mrs. [X] because I feel the methods you use to obtain information for your cynical newspaper articles, and how you try to use your comics to get at people, is reporting that is below the belt.

Bugging people's phones is against the law. Anyone who hires snitches and snoops to invade others' privacy has no right to whine if their victims are displeased.

Why don't you just shorten the name of your rag to the Star, because that's what you are.

Fortunately, California has anti-stalking laws. Of course, a newspaper editor who doesn't understand balanced reporting or fairness can't be expected to grasp privacy rights.

Wonder how long before someone gives you a dose of your own medicine, and how you will like it?

Number Three: Dear Crybaby:

You have a lot of nerve to whine and cry about readers' reactions to your comic strips. You snivel that it upsets you when a subscriber complains about the contents of your paper.

Many of us feel comic strips are supposed to amuse, not to push your ideas down our throats, hurt our feelings, nor make people angry and resentful.

You forget, sire: Are you responsible for the contents of your newspaper? Are you aware that other people will react to what you publish?

If freedom of expression means you can publish whatever you want, it also means we readers have the right to dislike it and tell you so. You are a big boy, Mr. Editor. If you can dish it out, you should be able to take it.

As Harry Truman said: If you can't take the heat, get out of the kitchen!

A LACK OF UNDERSTANDING:

Most readers don't know or understand the ins and outs of newspaper work. Editors clearly need to explain more about the business. For instance, readers don't understand about libel and the legal concerns of convicting a suspect in print before his or her day in court—or publicly tar-and-feathering "criminals." Following is an example letter.

We are writing this letter to tell you how tired we are of seeing your paper refer to criminals as "alleged," "suspected," etc. when they have been caught in the act. We are referring specifically to your stories in yesterday's and today's editions about the two punks who took a car at knifepoint and were subsequently killed during the pursuit by sheriff's deputies.

At least today's story says one of these had a reputation as a troublemaker with the deputies at the substation, but that is the piece's only redeeming feature.

You don't seem to understand that bad people are bad people and need to be labeled as such—especially when they are pursued by authorities during flight from their crime. They are not "alleged" or "suspected," especially when they crash a car that was stolen at knifepoint and they are found in it. How the heck do you think they got there? By magic?

One reason the youth of our society are confused about moral issues is because the media casts doubt upon the guilt of parties whose guilt is obvious to the densest individual in our society.

UNCONSCIOUS JERK:

It sometimes seems the people that get the angriest are the least educated. The following letter blistered the editor for a personal column explaining that a column by syndicated columnist Dr. Peter Gott had offended several Chinese people and that the newspaper possibly "fell asleep at the wheel" and shouldn't have published it. There were numerous misspellings and punctuation mistakes (included below) in the original letter:

What a unctuous jerk you are. holding some poor under-paid and overworked "editor" up to ridicule in your miserable, feckless, badly written Sunday column on the editorial page. first place, what is this "dear editor"—what unction to begin with. It is pompous and self serving.

Further, if you wanted to apologize for the column, write a short apology in italics and drop it into the middle of gott s column, putting the blame where it belongs—dr. gott. After all that column (bad and unfunny as it was) had already been passed by several editors on the syndicate before it got to your man.

You are a poor excuse for a newspaper editor.

MORE GOTT:

Following is a different perspective, but just as personal.

I am one of the people who got a tremendous kick out of Dr. Gott's anti-smoking column, and I am a quarter Chinese. For every hyper-sensitive, narrow-minded whiner who complained to you there are probably thousands who understood the satire of Mr. Gott's work. He is an even better writer than I give him credit for. You should "go asleep at the wheel" more often. (Shame on you for using the cliché.)

A well-known magazine did a reader analysis a few years ago in which they learned that people who grew up on *Sesame Street* usually have an attention span no longer than 10 lines (newspaper column) and unless something starts jumping around, like a Muppet, that's it for them. Furthermore, they don't understand satire at all. Dr. Gott didn't fail at satire as you say, you and your whiner-readers failed at understanding it.

I think you are a disgrace to journalism. You failed to stand behind your writer. You side with wimps, twits and political correctness perverts, when no doubt the bulk of your audiences is likely made up of intelligent people. You pretend you're sorry the column slipped through, but you're really passing the buck, trying to get yourself off the hook, trying to save face. If you had any journalistic sense at all, you'd dump the little-brains' letters into the trash. If you had any sense of values, you'd tell them to try adulthood, try to be a real person. They fancy themselves as "do-gooders," and write to you because you give all the indications in your so-so copy that you, too, are a "do-gooder" and will give them some "do-good" press, when in reality you are contributing to demoralization and common sense of the Nation. You haven't solved any problem with your anti-Gott column, you have made yourself part of the problem.

Only the Chinese populations on the West Coast got upset. Are these Chinese sympathetic to the communist cause of "The Fortune-Cookie Land?" If so, what are they doing in this country? The bunch of them should be immediately deported so they can get out of their BMWs and Lexus' and back on bicycles and really enjoy human rights.

You should read "A Nation of Victims" and you'd see who these enemies to intellectuality really are and how corrupt they are in thought. But then, you're not so uncorrupt in thought yourself by throwing your lot in with these numnums and left-wing loonies. Shame on you again.

If you have to watch PBS at all, you should break away from re-runs of *Sesame Street* and watch *Frontline* and in the interim, practice upgrading your interpretation skills.

Cordially,

FRANK OBSERVER:
"What do the following have in common? Watering a post, castrating eunuchs, talking to a stone, and carrying water in a sieve. As explained in the Dictionary of Quotations, they are amusing similes from literature used as examples of futile expenditures of energy. Add to that list 'collecting money after winning a small claims court decision.'" The preceding four sentences were the lead to a column talking about a handyman who was paid, but never completed the work agreed upon. He was taken to small

claims court and ordered to re-pay the money. But, collecting the money became a nightmare. The following letter came from "Frank Observer."

You don't know me, but I know you. I'm an employee. That's why I won't sign my name to this letter. That would put my job at risk.

This is about your column. Your columns generally are terrible. They are shallow and solipsistic; badly written; off the wall; no thought given to them before you write.

Today's is one of the worst, relating something that is highly personal, an incident wherein you tried to get a job done cheaply by an unlicensed handy man instead of a licensed union carpenter.

Then you blame the courts because you can't collect your judgment. The courts aren't collection agencies. Courts adjudicate matters and decide who is right and who is wrong. You won that round. Collecting is a different matter. What do you expect the courts to do, put him in jail, send a Marshall to his house and make him write a check?

Before I flunked out, I spent a year at Harvard Law School. The professor there said: "You can sue the Pope for bastardy, but you can't collect."

Next point: Who cares that you were fommoxed [*sic*] by a tinker? Readers have their own problems and they don't want to hear about those of an executive of a chain of newspapers, especially when that executive should know better.

W. C. Fields said it best: "You can't cheat an honest man."

As you have discerned, I work for wages. But there's more to it than that: I want to be proud of the newspaper I work for. Your Sunday columns greatly diminish that job satisfaction.

So, step aside and give that precious space to someone who can write. Or maybe sell the space for an ad. Advertisers pay premium prices for space on the editorial or op-ed pages.

Chapter Twelve

A Lack of Clarity

The front-page headline screamed:
SPECIAL REPORT
Horror hits home
Five die in gunman's bloody rampage

The readout headline followed: First mass shooting in county: Unemployed Ventura aerospace engineer kills three people at state EDD office in Oxnard and an Oxnard police officer before being shot to death by pursuing officers following a half-hour chase.

The newspaper told the story of a thirty-three-year-old man who had long hair and a scraggly beard. On that day he wore a dark coat and tie. He carried a 12-gauge shotgun in a brown box.

Alan Winterbourne had been unemployed almost seven years.

A man in the unemployment office said, "He didn't say anything. He just started firing at the employees."

A woman said, "All I know is a lone gunman came up from behind me, went to the counter, pulled out a rifle and just started shooting.

"To me, he looked like someone who had filed a claim and had been turned down or something.

"When he started shooting there was total silence. He didn't say a word. Nobody screamed."

Winterbourne was an unemployed computer engineer. He took deliberate aim at employees who were helping customers with claims.

Workers hid under desks or ran for the door.

One employee first saw a computer screen explode, and then a male coworker dropped to the floor and went into convulsions. Then there were more popping sounds, and she was also hit.

Another employee threw her body over a wounded coworker. She was then shot.

After the rampage, the shooter's sister said he was "…despondent but not to the point of being stupid. He's a pacifist, a great kid."

He was scheduled to baby-sit her young son minutes after the shootings. He never showed up and his sister worried.

"I kept hearing shooting and reloading and reloading," an office supervisor said.

The above excerpts from the newspaper account were riveting reading. But maybe even more interesting to some, scary and unnerving to many reporters and editors, was the story of what Alan Winterbourne did moments before the horror began.

The newspaper's editorial page editor wrote a front-page story, as part of the coverage package, detailing that time frame. Following are excerpts.

On Thursday morning, Alan Winterbourne, unemployed since 1986, left home with a cardboard box filled with seven years' worth of letters, job applications and help-wanted ads.

On the cover of a 3-by-5 notebook in which he had kept a meticulous log of his job search, he wrote: "At least 1 contact a day 5 days a week 2/14/86–12/2/93."

On this day, he apparently decided his long job search was over.

Winterbourne drove to the newspaper, where he dropped off a box in the lobby and delivered a separate envelope containing what he must have thought were key documents—job performance reviews from his former employer, his resignation from the company, a transcript from his unemployment compensation benefit appeals hearing, and a letter to his congressman.

The envelope was addressed to me, the opinion page editor. As he handed it over, he explained it contained "some documents about unemployment" and said he would call back later in the day or Friday to discuss it.

Less than a half-hour later, Alan Winterbourne entered the Oxnard Employment Development Department office carrying a handgun and loaded shotgun. He opened fire on employees there.

What drove Winterbourne to the EDD office? The documents he placed in the envelope—apparently in the knowledge they would be used as the basis to tell the story—detail a grievance with the office over a denial of benefits.

In Winterbourne's cardboard box were 288 rejection letters from firms he had sought work over the past six-plus years.

GOING DEEP ON DEATH:

Newspaper journalists are often instructed to write stories that can be understood by an eighth-grader.

KISS—Keep It Simple Stupid—is a good rule. The same applies for letters to the editor, although those who write and read letters might be writing, reading, and thinking on a bit higher level (ninth grade maybe?). Whatever, the following unsigned letter contained far more substance than the typical rant.

We must all pass through the great transition, cross the inevitable threshold at some time. Life strives to make its duration as long as possible. But man is more than a living entity. Man is a thinking, active, creative being. When these faculties and powers are taken from man, he retrogresses. His cycle as a human being is completed. If then, under such circumstances he desires transition, why should he be denied it?

If the soul survives, which most everyone believes, man's transition by euthanasia will not in any way affect the soul's continuation elsewhere. Man then, in resorting to euthanasia, has not wrongly taken life by requesting that it cease. Life itself, for him, has malfunctioned and the present chapter of the book is closed. Why wait and prolong the agony of something that is no longer functional for oneself or for others, thus mocking its former goodness?

Death is an incorrect name because neither the physical body nor the psychic body ever ceases to exist. In both cases, they both return to their basic forms of existence. What actually occurs is a change, a transfer of position from one state of continued existence to another. Transition does not bring with it eternal suffering or does it carry forward endless amusement, it provides a doorway to opportunity, an initiatory portal of hope, a gateway toward eventual reconciliation between ourself and the greater mind of God. Transition is an integral part of the scope of our life and cannot ultimately be avoided by anyone.

There are many individuals who virtually vegetate once their mind is gone, and they are of advanced age—there is no hope except further deterioration. Therefore, in such cases, the afflicted person remains just an animated mass. We can also mention the futile use of physicians, medical equipments and facilities that could be put to greater use, in saving lives that would be restored to activity and enjoyment of life.

There is likewise no cosmic reason one must endure for years the great pain of an incurable disease. What kind of cosmic justice would it be if there was a cosmic mandate that men and women must endure such suffering? Karma is not intentionally punitive. It does not seek to punish for a violation of its laws. It is not a retribution for a wrong act. It is merely the law of cause and effect, and impersonal in its function. Therefore, karma would not impose a penalty in an act of euthanasia. When a person is in horrible pain for a long period of time, then euthanasia may seem quite acceptable.

Admittedly this is a controversial subject. Some are displeased with the thought of euthanasia. Some may feel emotional and shocked by its use. Conversely, there will be others who will find humane justification in its use.

FOR APRIL FOOLS:

Letters to the editor are sometimes so confusing it is anyone's guess what the author is trying to say. Sometimes they can be salvaged, rewritten, and published. But most don't see the light of day. Editors sometimes wonder about the mental stability of such letter writers, especially if there is a progression of deterioration of letters. The following four letters were received in the same envelope with "Super Info Being" as the return address. The letters all had different dates and one letter was addressed to "April Fools."

March 23: OK guys, here's an easy one, on this total act of discrimination against smokers. I would really like to know how anyone can test for second-hand smoke. Even more ridiculous, what about the effect of second-hand smoke on a fetus? Give me a break!

I think this is all a lie! Gasses, chemicals, radiation and much more than that is in the air. Can anyone explain those effects?

I wonder could they be the ones testing for smoke—blaming smokers!

How much poison is sprayed daily in the air and ground just to kill weeds? This is only one example of the deadly gasses that are in the air, more than if you smoke.

Tell me again, us smokers are the cause of problems?

Why doesn't your newspaper publish these test findings and how they were found? I sure would like to see this. When is the public going to join together and not stand for this any longer?

Also, there is so much talk of crime and burglaries! I have never seen any form of trouble in years. I feel very safe. I haven't talked to anyone who is afraid.

I think there is something wrong being attempted. Like total control of another—brain washing!

Fear is how it is done and the media sure seems to only go out of its way to constantly spread and write of it. Why?

It's obvious to me—to be a society of two classes—those who give orders and those who take orders! Kinda like slaves and slave drivers! And you call this an answer?

March 29: Is it only me who can plainly see that the only crime needed to worry about is being done by USA government employees? Those with titles of senator and congressman—or drug dealers, thieves and rapists. They are all the same.

I think it is time to change this game. Those who tell others what they can or can not do should be taken out of control. If not, all will lose.

This system is so out of whack and that is a fact. Officials must be getting a good laugh at the public. To allow others the control of their lives, money and property is beyond me.

What is it going to take before humans stop this organized group of criminals called the government?

Wake up people. USA is now in the progress of what's called a "holocaust" if no one is aware. It is sad that acts as these are never recognized until after the fact.

Well, this indigent is not afraid to call it not just as I see it, but as it is. I am not afraid to call thieves, thieves and liars, liars. And this is the type who's running this show.

The future is now and soon to be no more if people don't wake up! What a waste. But I guess this is what's meant to be. After all, they wrote the book…didn't they?

Good luck to all. It's needed!

April 1: OK! Now I'll try a different approach. Could it be you powerful, rich men are too afraid to respond to me? You certainly haven't responded to my letters. Well, I'm not afraid of any of you or your lies. I know your ways.

You can discredit me all you want, but it won't stop me. The longer you ignore me, the more points I score, not you!

I guess it is tough to enter a game you know you'll lose! If time is what you are betting on, I've got much more than any of you!

Again, let the game begin. Put your mouth where your money is!

April 8: The "Interstate Commerce Act," which was passed Feb. 4, 1887 by Congress, states: "The Interstate Commerce Commission executes and enforces the act in the public interest, promotes safe service and conditions, prevents unjust rates and discriminatory practice."

Does this still exist?

If so, how would I contact them? If not so, why not?

My reason for this information is it's time those who set and raise utility prices be held accountable for their actions.

I have a few questions to ask and they won't or can't answer.

If I receive my usual response to letters I send as this, which is none at all, I promise I'll find it somewhere!

It's time the public knows they pay for gifts given to them.

Also, why should anyone worry, let alone pay for "flood control." For years I have been encouraged to think there is a drought so why so much emphasis on flood control? Or how is raising water rates going to produce more water?

The greed is getting too obvious. I'm certainly not going to ignore criminal acts as these. If you think by ignoring me, these matters will go away, wrong for U! I speak of this and much more to a lot of taxpayers who are as fed up as I am!

By ignoring me you only prove you can't, won't or don't want to answer my questions. Why?

I know I have no proof on paper (yet) of what I know, but I also know you have no proof or purpose for water rates (and probably more).

You can bet on this! You know how and where to find me.

Chapter Thirteen

Don't You Know I'm Clever?

The American Society of Newspaper Editors meets once a year. They talk a lot about how well they are doing across America, and even talk about how newspapers could improve. How much talk turns into action is a good question.

Most years the meeting is in Washington, D.C. There's a certain importance about meeting in the nation's capitol—important editors and important politicians.

One year a reception for about 700 editors was scheduled at Vice President Al Gore's home on the grounds of the Naval Observatory.

The editor's young son found out about his dad being an invited guest. A week before the meeting he asked:

"Get something while you're back there."

"What do you mean," the editor asked the ten-year-old.

"Take something as a 'memento' from the house."

"I'm not going to rip him off!" the editor said.

But once he was there, waiting in line to get his photo taken with a beardless Big Al and Tipper, something came over him.

Following is a column of the experience, written upon his return. It was titled: **Ripping off Al Gore.**

My ten-year-old son was impressed when I told him I was going to visit Vice President Al Gore's home in Washington, D.C.

"Wow," he said. "Do you know him?"

"Not exactly. But I've been invited to a reception at his house."

"Bring me something back," he demanded.

"How about a bar of soap or a towel from the bathroom?" he asked.

I wanted to shout, "Sure, no problem." But all I could think about was getting caught and the morning headline:

California editor arrested, jailed after stealing from VP Gore's toilet.

There were other mind-boggling scenarios, like why a ten-year-old wanted a bar of soap or a towel from the vice president of the United States. After all, his Naval Observatory home isn't exactly Motel 6.

It was obvious he didn't want to be clean. Ten-year-old boys like dirt...it has something to do with keeping girls away.

I gave up wondering why he wanted me to rip off Big Al. Still, I knew I had to bring something back, even if it didn't come from Tipper's John. My mission was clear. Don't break the law, but impress the kid by giving him something to impress his friends.

"How about a blade of grass from the lawn?" I asked.

"Oh, that's cool, I guess," he said. He obviously thought I was a wimp.

"I'll get something," I said, and off to Washington I went.

The night in question I was among about 700 invitees attending the American Society of Newspaper Editors' annual convention. When my friend, an editor from Ohio, and I arrived, we got off the bus and walked through a security checkpoint to the lawn.

A half-hour of small talk later, we got in line to tour a part of the house, and to meet the Gores.

We were behind a chatter-box from Canada.

"Newt [Gingrich] did a great job speaking yesterday," she gushed. "The vice president was OK today, but don't you think the Republicans will win?...Who do you think Dole's running mate will be?...I wonder what he's going to say tomorrow when he speaks to us?"

She went on and on and on without a breath, or a requested response. She wouldn't shut up.

But it soon became clear she would be useful in my mission. As we entered a side door to the residence, we came to two partially opened doors.

Quick as a flash, she darted into the one marked "Powder Room." She came back with a small, heavy-paper hand-towel embossed with the seal of the vice president of the United States.

It was too good to be true.

Maybe I could bring my ten-year-old a towel (albeit of the paper-and-hand variety).

I played dumb. "Where'd you get that?" I asked. "From there," she said, pointing to the powder room.

"Could you get me one?" I asked.

As she walked away she shouted back: "Sure, no problem."

TURNING WEIRD:

Editorial cartoonists often have a bizarre sense of humor. Two local cartoonists offered "opinions" following an earthquake. One showed a man sleeping in a tent, his wife still in the house. The caption read: "Fear of aftershocks? Heck no. I'm out here because of the Bobbitt verdict" [a woman who cut off her husband's member]. The other cartoon showed strange looks on the faces of three people, with a doctor suggesting: "It's being called either the 'California Stare,' or 'Aftershock Startle' or the 'Fault Frown.'" The following letter addressed the cartoons.

I have no way of knowing with certainty whether your staff or you have noticed your cartoonists have turned weird—even for cartoonists. It is written in the "Sacred Book of Journalist Rights," that unlike other workers in the vineyard of the Fourth Estate, cartoonists are explicitly exempt from the rule that two psychiatrists must agree on their mental soundness (not the psychiatrists, but the cartoonists).

Sad to say, but the last three or four cartoons since the Big Milk Shake have been pieces grotesquely ridiculing people affected mentally by the shakes. Now, you know, such behavior would be regarded by the average person as akin to passing wind at a family funeral.

Would you have a quiet chat with them, when it is possible (soon), and run them down on the appropriate etiquette in such matters?

Anyway, their cartoons frequently pass the test of humor and sense with little to spare. Sometimes their stuff is just opaque. I think they may unluckily have entered a weird world of unacceptable imagination due to that same quake!

Of course all this blather from a layman may merely be confirmation to them of their talent.

CONFIGURE THIS!

Most letter writers aren't funny, but many think they are. The following letter came at a time when press configuration and capacity concerns dictated a newspaper that wasn't consistent in "booking"—features, pages, and sections being placed in the same order or space on a daily basis. Even though the letter writer had legitimate concerns, the criticism was hard to take because of the sarcastic humor.

At last I think I've figured out how you put the paper together. I just want confirmation.

First, it's my theory you print one copy of each page. Next, you throw all the pages into a medium-sized, wire dog cage. After that, you turn a powerful fan on the cage until all the pages fly. You turn off the fan, let the pages settle and there you have it—the order for that day. It must be the way you put together your newspaper.…A more disorganized paper I have never seen.

STEPHEN AWARD WINNER:

The following was submitted as an "official" press release, but was obviously tongue-in-cheek—except for the believed bias or message of the letter writer.

The local chapter of the American Family Association has unanimously selected its "Stephen Award" winner. The award is given to the local media source that demonstrated the most anti-Christian bias throughout the prior year. Your newspaper is this year's winner.

We sincerely hope in the coming year you will extend tolerance to include the Christian community. It is our hope that in the future all the facts are reported on an issue and the merits of it will be decided by the people. The news media is supposed to be an open marketplace of ideas, not a marketing entity for an ideology.

THE BEST OF THE BEST:
The following letter is absolutely one of the best of all time. It references the Tonya Harding/Nancy Kerrigan Olympic shenanigans.

I am enclosing a copy of a telegram I sent to Tonya Harding the day she was scheduled to skate [in the Olympics]. I am wondering if this was appropriate or not.

TONYA HARDING
CARE U.S. OLYMPIC TEAM
LILLEHAMMER [NORWAY]

BREAK A LEG.

A BRAIN-DEAD NEWSPAPER:
Some letter writers are very clever in suggesting alternative uses for a newspaper.

Isn't it about time to pull the plug on that brain-dead newspaper of yours? Ever since it was improved, the quality of the entire thing has steadily diminished. At first, I tried calling editors of various departments to call attention to my grievances, but they always passed the buck.

I waited to see if there would be any improvements, but it grows continually worse.

For example, there is always a blank streak down the left or right hand column of every edition. I know there is special terminology for left and right in journalism, but you guys wouldn't know that. You never read the paper. Just to break the monotony, there is occasionally a black streak through the middle of the column.

Of course my all-time favorite is the New York Times crossword puzzle. Part of it is usually missing, and the print is so small no one can read it. I happen to be a Times crossword addict, and have called so often about that. You would not know this, but it was to your advantage when the crossword puzzle appeared in the classified section. At least it had me glancing through the section.

Now, I gloss over the editorials and letters, but never find a reason to look inside, therefore, ignoring all of the paid advertisers. You are so busy beating your drum for advertising, that you don't realize you defeated your purpose.

Now you may wonder why, if I dislike the newspaper so vehemently, I continue to subscribe. The truth is that I have a paper-trained puppy and the newspaper serves her purposes quite well.

My most recent favorite was the past week, where you showed a picture of a teen-aged girl assisting an older woman, and in bold type, you wrote…PORES TEA.

Pull the plug!

WINCH VERSUS WRENCH VERSUS WENCH:
The ad read: Electric Wench, $100. (805) 555-5555.

Another word that should be posted on a bulletin board for your ad writers is "winch." It is always spelled "wench" in your ads. Wench pertains to a girl or maiden. Or did this ad mean "wrench?"

Chapter Fourteen

Long-winded and Lost

The young editor had just gotten the opportunity of a lifetime. He had toiled for the past six years as a rising editor at an 85,000-circulation daily newspaper, the past two years as managing editor.

He was offered a job as editor-publisher at a small daily some fifty miles north in Central California.

Yes, it was a much smaller newspaper, but he'd be in charge. Or at least he thought he would. And he'd get a $15,000-a-year increase. Heady stuff.

Wide-eyed, he packed his bags, not knowing the amount of idiocy he would soon be facing.

Once on board, a reception for the community at the newspaper was planned.

A week before the gathering, he got a taste of the importance of being a publisher of a small newspaper. The phone rang late one night. The women's toilet had backed up and a mess had to be cleaned up, as well as a toilet unclogged, before workers arrived the next morning.

He went to the office, plunger and mop in hand.

Once fixed, he made his first executive-level decision.

The production manager, who was actually in charge of facilities and was with the young publisher the night of the plunger-and-mop campaign, informed his boss the reason for the backflow was twofold: 1) sanitary napkins flushed down the toilet rather than placed in the provided bucket with a foot-flip-step top. 2) Hand towels flushed, rather than thrown in the trash.

He didn't have a clue how to address the sanitary napkin problem. But he had an answer for the paper towel problem. Hand dryers.

Still, that problem and decision paled to the concern that came up at the community reception.

Everything was going well, when he heard a commotion across the room. A Mexican-American visitor was ranting, raving, and animatedly waving his hands at the newspaper controller, a twenty-six-year-old woman with long blonde hair and pale white skin.

The contrasts were aplenty.

He quickly made his way over to the discussion and asked if he could help.

The visitor said the female employee had "disparaged my people."

"What do you mean?" the editor-publisher asked.

"She said she was 'just a bean counter.'"

Well, the young woman certainly wasn't in Kansas anymore.

She was a Yooper! That's what people from the Upper Peninsula of Michigan are called.

It isn't the most diverse part of the country. As an example, this young woman only ate Taco Bell food after she turned twenty and moved to California.

She meant nothing by her comment. She was trying to be funny. She was an accountant, and they have long been called "bean counters."

Some letter writers fancy themselves as novelists or pen pals. Their letters are either long or come in a series, or both. They are also often just as tragic as short, one-page letters. Following is the correspondence from some lost souls [the first five from the same person, sent over a long period of time].

Number One: Dear Sirs,

This is a written request for a hearing contesting the order of correction in citation #1111111 and conclusions of the citation and Surety Company of the Pacific payment to the Smiths' and amount to the Jones' that was paid without my agreement.

There is an implied agreement between a surety company and a contractor when a bond is purchased to act in good faith to that agreement, and any payment made by the surety company against the bond must be in observance of reasonable commercial standards. This requires that the contractor agree to such payment or that it is a result of an order of a court or a Contractors State License Board Judge.

This is not the case in both of these payments, which I object to, one in the amount, and no payment was due to the Smiths'.

Let me first state, before reviewing both jobs, that I am a victim of this very unbelievable crime of radio electronics in my ear areas placed there by the federal government in 1956.

The electronics robs all thought, sedates the brain partly, induces thoughts, speaks with quick computer voices 24 hours a day without stop, attempting to alter thinking, and has the capacity to alter organ function.

This caused sweating attacks from 1964 to 1988, causing great suffering and effect on my life. All this happened, of course, with some people in state government having knowledge.

I was in a number of mental hospitals because of this from 1986 to 1988 for periods of stay (induced paranoia).

They started speaking to me in 1989 through this and nobody has halted this crime yet.

The Supreme Court of California denied my writ of habeas corpus in February of this year, so I wait and ask you to help me, a contractor who is a victim of this serious crime and violation. We are all as free as every one of us is free.

I hope to obtain removal soon and be a free person. With that I hope to receive a monetary amount that will reflect what has happened and the great violation of my rights for

36-plus years. With that, I will probably become involved with construction in a much larger way.

Briefly, Mr. and Mrs. Jones' project was not completed by me because of what was going on at the time in this crime of radio electronics. My judgment as to cost to complete was $2,500.

The Smiths' project problem was agreed to be corrected by the Smiths' for a payment of $3,000 by me to them as payment in full to solve the problem at that project. This was done with full knowledge of Mr. Doe of the State Contractors License Board, with whom I spoke many times with about this.

Sincerely,

Number Two: This is a request of the Supreme Court of California for an immediate issuance of either a writ of mandate or a writ of habeas corpus to order removal of the very illegal and unconstitutional presence of radio electronics in me.

Also, to order removal if they are in my children or my ex-wife.

As described in my request dated May 12, the presence is very inhumane and injurious mentally and psychologically and must be ordered by the court to be removed immediately.

Sincerely,

Number Three: At this time, I would like to add the police chief as a respondent in my request for either a writ of mandate or a writ of habeas corpus, to remove radio electronics from me.

I lived in the city, leaving for brief periods of time, from 1957 to 1988. I believe I had radio electronics in me all during that period and this was known by the Police Department.

Because of the length of time this great violation of my rights and person, and the nature of the violation, the Santa Paula Police Department has a duty to correct and stop this very illegal presence of radio electronics in me and also any member of my immediate family, if it is in them.

Sincerely,

Number Four: Dear Sir,

In this letter I am asking for your help in my struggle to remove radio electronics from my ear areas placed there in 1956 and requesting a continuance in CSLB Case #1111111.

I am including a letter I sent to the California State License Board; please read.

As stated on page two of that letter, the radio electronics robs all thought which greatly violates my right of private thought, a 4th Amendment right.

Also, due to this capacity, if a hearing were held, my right as stated in the 5th Amendment to be a witness against myself would be greatly violated.

Because of this, the fact it slows the brain and its presence in me causes duress, a hearing can not be held since it violates my person and due process.

A fair hearing, any hearing, prior to removal of this by either the federal, state or local government is unconstitutionally impossible. A hearing in this case must be postponed till it can be conducted constitutionally.

This is a great violation of my person and rights, and a threat to all persons in construction. Freedom and rights should be the foremost goal of the California State Contractor's License Board to correct and safeguard. This is what you must do.

So I ask for your help and resources to help me gain my freedom from these people.

All persons must stand for freedom and against this in construction.

Once removed, the amount in dispute in this will seem very small in comparison to what monetarily is due from the government as a result of this since 1956.

The presence of the illegal and unwanted radio electronics, which also may be in my children, in this state can not be allowed.

This is my belief and also the belief of everyone in construction today. This is what is important and a 9-1-1 for persons in construction.

Sincerely,

Number Five: Your Honor,

This is a request of you to extend the filing period of my petition for a writ of certiorari beyond the normal 90-day period and to extend this period an additional 60 days.

This was asked of the court in my petition previously filed. The California Court of Appeal ruled and June 20 is the 130th day after that ruling.

As stated in my petition, the devices greatly affect me in many ways. They cause duress, sedation, memory blockage and loss affecting my ability to act as my own lawyer greatly.

Because this is so illegal and unconstitutional, and affects my mental abilities greatly, the extension must be approved because just and fair allowance of extension, but more importantly the very great need of the United States Supreme Court and you as individual Justices to rule to free me and my children or ex-wife, if it is in them, from this radio electronic enslavement, which you must do by issuing either a temporary injunction or restraining order.

The documents have been re-mailed to the Supreme Court.

You must extend the filing period as requested and more importantly immediately issue a temporary injunction or temporary restraining order in this unbelievable violation of my person, rights, life and property and if my children or ex-wife, them also.

I believe a first payment of $500,000 is just and very needed to secure privacy.

Sincerely,

LORD HELP US ALL:

To Whom It May Concern.

What I'm about to tell you is not only unbelievable but so bizarre you'll question my sanity. But each and every sentence is true. I have documented evidence of every statement.

1980—About 14 years ago my husband associated with a guy who was known as a "computer person" (knowledgeable about systems, i.e., payback systems, setting up people so they hear hypnotism for x amount of time to pay them back for something). Yes, there are real people doing these things. This is the only way I can think of that what I am going to tell you happened. I have since seen this person in and around my home at 3 and 4 in the morning. It wasn't my fault my husband did what he did.

1982 to 1984—Now, this person decided to go to the extreme when he had his own "paybacks." He volunteered me for an implant. He signed up for an experimental surgery for his "wife." I've seen her; she could be my double, only thinner. The experiment could be conducted by none other than the CIA doctors. His "wife" would be a prototype for the first implant in a human that could actually communicate with a larger system, i.e., decipher, have imagery, have mapping abilities, etc. But his "wife" became another person. Under heavy hypnotism, she was taken in and the delicate micro surgery was done; him and her aforehand agreeing to this saying she "didn't want to know" when the surgery was done because she was afraid only of that, but not the results. Since she and her husband were both technicians in the computer field, what better subjects.

1985—Suddenly depression hit our home. Our 12-year-old dog turned up missing. A baby was lost. My grandfather one day just walked into the hospital, checked in and died that night. Depression was so intense. I'd stay in the same robe and nightgown for four or five days, without even getting dressed.

"I'm Mary Smith," I'd "hear" someone say about every three or four hours. "Well, she doesn't live here and go away," I found myself saying out loud. Yet I "heard" her outside my windows, she'd call on the phone, she'd wake me up at night. Before I knew it, I was in a world of horrible hypnotism. I couldn't think or function. Trying to hold a conversation or put a sentence together was impossible. This went on for two years before I reported it to police (I was told if I told anyone they would put them through it).

1987—Officers Black and Green came to our apartment to answer a complaint I made about "hearing things" and to look for any electrical equipment that could be responsible. Found nothing. "Seek professional help."

I "hear" the CIA and FBI looking for someone. Someone that was important to them. Why would they be looking for me? I'm under hypnotism so horrible I'm afraid to go out of my home or even hold my daughter.

1988—Suddenly a hypnotist who is trying to "bring me out of it" gets through in her computer personality (I found out later that was the only way they could communicate with me). I feel beautiful and radiate inner peace. I feel like a wonderful, loving grandmother has taken me in her arms to nurture and care about. I feel like this for about four months. Although the voices are still there, I'm talking to the "Hispanic Lil," an FBI agent/hypnotist. "Who are you talking to?" I keep hearing from whom I called "Ms. Manners." She was the "voice" that constantly badgered, took self esteem away with hypnotism, etc.

The CIA and FBI systems put a "computer personality" of this loving person into my "minute instant system." I'm saying "hearing" loosely because it's not like anything a person hears. All of a sudden I would just know something, usually something I wouldn't have any way of knowing or something I thought at the time was someone trying to get me to believe things from a science fiction movie.

1990—Horrible hypnotism again. They tell me they killed pop (my grandfather). I'm living a walking hell. I can't even tell anyone about it. They'll "do it" to anyone I tell. (Pop's system is still there at his house.)

1991—I finally tell a good friend. "I think it has something to do with computers." Can she help me? Her roommate is into computers; will she talk with him for me and see if there is any way for someone to do this to me?

In December, her boyfriend blows her away with a shotgun, then himself. "See what happens," I'm told. Her "system" is still there, too.

1992—Constant hypnotism, but not as bad for some reason.

1993—I tell my best friend, and she begins to hear the same as me. Every day she comes over crying "I can't take this anymore." We go to the police and FBI again. "Seek professional help," they both say. I "see" system at police station (where it is wired into the station).

I got "knocked to my knees" from some kind of force

physically and literally dropping me to my knees (at the police station).

In East Park there are two systems under the picnic benches. I found out there is one everywhere I go. I literally get my polarization reversed and it effects me physically.

The most horrible three months of my life.

Why won't the police help? This guy bragged about what he did to me to a friend of a friend. Detailed. I can identify him. We are not crazy. Mind control. That's what all these systems are!

Go to doctor and get X-ray. Tiny black dots in a complete circle around the top of my head turn up. "It's nothing," the doctor says. I can "hear" the system there. I go to my shrink. Other than the haloperidol injection I get every two weeks he puts me on oral 20 mil a day. I can't stop crying.

The CIA is back. They're doing something that makes a hissing sound. They say they're "tripping" on us. They thought I knew. Knew what? I ask out loud. Your system is trying to kill you. A new system. I'm being depolarized a lot now (it feels like all your molecules are being split and pulled apart in my head).

I thought these were real people I "heard." They begin telling me what all these (by now they'd counted 19) systems did and why and what they are (were) doing. "These are bombs," some of them said. "We thought you could operate the larger system." They'd go from one system to another and I could hear them turning off (or tripping) the systems. "These are going to hurt," referring to the ones implanted on the backs of my eyes. They did when they were tripped.

I keep trying to call CIA in Los Angeles. Getting no-where—recording. I'll go down there to the CIA office in Norwalk. It was an empty room with a phone machine and recorded messages.

I call the FBI in Los Angeles. "There's never been a CIA on the West Coast," they said. "Funny, it's in the phone book," I said. They told me to call the CIA in Washington, D.C. Information gives me Virginia every time. But the CIA's in D.C. I know it is!

My brother is a CIA agent in Iraq and he works from Washington, D.C. What's wrong with my phone? Again (tap found in July), phone company can't find tap now. Someone is using phone to fax. People are calling saying they thought our number was a fax machine!

The CIA systems keep telling me "get help! You've got to get someone to believe you. Get a hold of the CIA, they'll help you."

Then nothing. I "hear" something like someone is "un-plugging" me. Then "jeering." Someone had sent in those CIA systems just in time to stop this little mother from blowing my head off. Not to mention the "caps" or "hats" as they call them that they "took elements" from. Fear made me forget and because I didn't want to believe it. They went through my system to "take elements" from my daughter and her friends. And tripped my son. He said they were "my people" so he was "confusing them, too."

1994—I went into the doctor's while he's on vacation to get his "fill in" to order a cat scan. He did, but out of own pocket. "Maybe this will make you quit all this," he said.

I got the CAT scan back, but no radiologist on there/phony results. It looks like an inside of a radio in my head.

"That guy" (John is his name) is still "digging" at sinuses and eyes with systems. My system sent out nitrous oxide to my other systems and froze them, but it doesn't last.

I go to the police. They won't let me make an updated report. I try to explain. They call mental health. Diane is still going through heavy hypnotism. Cries all the time. Mind bending and boggling.

Show CAT scan to shrink. "What's that around your skull?" Believes me, but what to do? If they don't know what these are, how do they go about dealing with them? Go back to police. Oh yeah, in August I got a threatening phone call. 9-1-1 wouldn't go through. I thought someone was going to come to my home and kill me. I call "0" and get Pac Bell. I tell them about the 9-1-1 incident and I wanted my phone checked again and when I dialed the police number and got through, they said they were working on the police lines. When I told them I was going there to make a report, she said for me to "make one on whoever is working on their lines too. They aren't Pac Bell and those are our lines. No requisition has ever been sent or filed."

All this seems like somebody has done something. You have to realize this mind control hypnotism works. If these people torturing me and my friend wanted you to believe something, you did. And if they want you to forget anything, you will.

But when the receptionist who refused to take another report at the police station got a gander at the CAT scan, she just about died. She still wouldn't let me talk to a detective or update my 1988 report even though I had pictures of "something ungodly" (as the technician called them) in my head. Know what she said? "Oh, go call the CIA about it."

And as I walked out, a black-and-white shined its spotlight at me from behind the station until I got in my car. When I went to find out who and why—they sped off.

When I "hear" things, you see, it all comes from the larger system that "John" controls. So someone sent systems in to save my life. The thing is, they're stolen. One of them (Hank), who is obviously CIA, went through my house with a system that built up energy from other systems. After that energy went around the world he could literally "blow up" a house or anything where another system was. John kept sending him in to kill me (my system). But he'd know who I was when he got to me. The entire attic where I live is copper wire strung out. It was another "Hank" that was making an "electrocution box" out of our home. But the other CIA "Hank" wouldn't give him the last "combination." I became very fond of the CIA Hank. But before I met him in my system he was a bit of a show off as to how many ways he could demolish things and people.

He was programmed to remember me and who I was and they couldn't take that away. So CIA, where are you now? Anyone try to call Washington, D.C. from here? One of their babies can't get home. Help!

In the CIA system, the original doctor was in there, along with another doctor I believe was the one who put in bombs and caps. The latter helped by finally breaking the system that was trying to kill me. They allowed themselves to be put in the system with all their knowledge that could help any given situation. They said they were allowed to be ripped off. If the original doctor was in there, I believe the CIA has been looking for me for a long time—about eight years. That's about when the larger system was stolen.

There is so much in nine years that has happened I can't begin to write it down. The reason I'm coming to you is to either put the story in the newspaper so the police might finally do something (like get in touch with the CIA and arrest this guy).

Or, to put a story in the paper that would bring people involved in that would go to the police (or fly to Washington, D.C.) with me.

I'm also coming to you for help in any way you think you can help. If you're planning on calling—you probably won't get me, as my phone has a tap on it and someone takes the calls when it rings. I don't know how it is set up, but I don't get all my calls. I have call waiting and my friends say they get a busy signal when they call all the time.

If you come over I'll show you my cat scan x-rays— Hubba Hubba! (Just kidding).

THE POET-GARDENER:

The following was addressed as an open letter to the police chief, newspaper editor, and U.S. Attorney General Janet Reno.

I am going to ask you to indulge this one, I hope, last letter. Yesterday, when I came to my room, from shopping, a brand new pack of cigarettes was gone. I remember them well, because I argued with myself before I went out, whether to take the one I had in my pocket or the unopened pack.

The man across the hall has been trying to bum cigarettes from me. His name is Gilbert, and I suspect his education has been largely in jails and prisons. He has a scar that runs by his neck below the ear that is ominous, to say the least.

He acts as if I should be indebited [*sic*] to him because he wants a smoke.

His roommate, Tim, whose nickname is "Wino," is always asking me to give him things, and one day, with the ruse that he wanted to give his 67-year-old mother a pair of earrings, he asked me to select three pair of clip-on types saying he would pay for them Saturday last, when he got his SSI check.

I set them aside, but Saturday came and went and now on the living room house downstairs he said the SSI had overpaid him and he was considering going into the ARC (recycling center) up on the coast.

Now, even realizing that Tim is a first-rate pathological liar, later I realized a connection, which may be entirely coincidental.

I lived up on the coast for nearly a year. In that time, a back-door thievery occurred in a yogurt shop, where the thief walked in and took $900 laying on a counter. I suspected a bicycle tramp named Chris who picked up cans only at night. He once told me that he was too smart for the cops. I thought he lived outside, but upon leaving, I discovered he was staying in the ARC.

About ten days ago, I passed Chris and his bicycle at the downtown mall. He stood staring at me, as I walked by.

Now there was another issue up on the coast. I went to the Mobile Recycling Center in the plaza there. The man who managed it was a strange fellow; he wears a leather vest every day and has a dirty looking dog. He never did like me, preferring this Chris fellow and two bums, both named Bill. One of the Bills told me he had a deal with supermarket teenage clerks who stole cigarette packs for him. These were not nice guys, they lived in a little car that the other Bill, a Canadian, bought, and lived by the state beach. They were filthy and drank, they told me, a gallon of vodka a day. Bill drove that car drunk all the time.

Finally, I figured out that the manager of this mobile unit had something else going on, he treated on occasion certain customers, coming in to sell cans with a high flutin' kind of respect. And because he would drink openly with the two Bills at his unit, I figured that maybe this unit would make a perfect way to railroad dope up and down the coast. Who would suspect a nasty old smelly recycling unit?

Now don't you find it terribly coincidental that here, a year later, I am living next door to the manager of the mobile recycling named Robby, who is shacked up with a

white woman named Martha? On the bus yesterday I asked
Robby if he knew the eccentric manager in the beach town.
He said he didn't, but I felt from his reaction that he did.
These guys make good money besides their hobby, at least
$11 an hour, so I have been told by the one in another
town.

That one was run by Reynolds Co., and I had to leave
there hurriedly because a punk just out of jail came too near
my camp, in a big black limousine with some other fellows
and threatened to do me in with a big baseball bat. I escaped to another area of the state immediately. The manager, Steve, lived up the road in some very, very expensive
apartments.

If you were going to move some crack or something
what better way than these smelly old recycling units? Up
and down the road.

On the coast, I once called to report the eccentric one in
their unit, I talked via his mobile phone, to the owner, who
said he thought we must have a personality conflict and
wasn't interested in my complaint.

So here I am living next to another one, and across the
hall is another person telling me he's planning to go live in
the Hotel ARC.

Makes me wonder.

P.S. When Gilbert moved, his so-called kinfolk who
helped him had those eyes of people who are hardened by
crime. Surely you know the look. Whores have that look
too. Tim recently got a haircut and shaved off his mustache.
Looks completely different. I will try to get his truck license number.

Chapter Fifteen

Credibility on All Fronts

Letter writers often lack credibility. But letter writers also regularly challenge media credibility, as the believability of reporters and editors is far too often suspect.

Comedian Chris Rock reportedly said, "You know the world is going crazy when the best rapper is a white guy, the best golfer is a black guy, the tallest guy in the NBA is Chinese, the Swiss hold the America's Cup, France is accusing the U.S. of arrogance, Germany doesn't want to go to war, and the three most powerful men in America are named Bush, Dick, and Colon."

I sometimes feel the same way—the world is going crazy—when it comes to ethics and journalism.

A review of the recent past proves plagiarism and lies in the media are far too common. That, however, isn't a recent phenomenon.

H. L. Mencken, the crusty newspaper columnist referenced earlier in this book, was an early leader of creative newspaper fiction. In 1917, he reported in the *New York Evening Mail* that President Millard Fillmore installed a bathtub in the White House. Fillmore was publicly criticized; bathing wasn't a priority at the time.

There was a problem, however. The story was a hoax. Mencken admitted it several years later, but it had become a "fact" and a part of history for many. Mencken's mischief was just that—a mischievous effort to see what he could stir up.

How many other reporters have made up facts, seeing what they could stir up? How many have crossed the accuracy line in the name of a better story? How many have stolen someone else's work?

It's easy in today's technologically advanced world to borrow someone else's words; they are at finger tips for the taking—some journalists just sign on, surf on, and steal away. The payoff can be high and the risk is usually low, especially if you are careful.

We live in a society where far too many believe it is OK to keep the $5 a fast-food restaurant clerk gives you in change when it should have been 50 cents. Others believe it is OK to lie to a spouse about infidelity, or sell a worthless product to an unsuspecting customer at a grossly inflated price.

So why not steal a few words—or make up a few? Ethics and morals come in many shades of gray. The temptation is real, alluring, and seductive. And we seem to be able to justify anything.

The price, however, is a heavy one to pay. In an industry that lives and dies on accuracy and truth telling, its main commodity—credibility—is often lost, or severely damaged.

The media has too many thieves and liars. Transgressions—politely termed "ethical lapses"—are common. Here's a look at some of the breeches of the credibility dam.

The 2003 *New York Times* Jayson Blair fiasco has been the most visible and damaging of the recent past. Plagiarism wasn't Blair's sin; it was deception. There is, understandably and understatedly, a significant credibility problem when a reporter becomes a creative nonfiction writer, taking bits and pieces of the truth and making up the rest.

In May, the *Times* wrote that Blair, "misled readers and *Times* colleagues with dispatches that purported to be from Maryland, Texas and other states, when often he was far away, in New York. He fabricated comments. He concocted scenes. He lifted material from other newspapers and wire services. He selected details from photographs to create the impression he had been somewhere or seen someone, when he had not. And he used these techniques to write falsely about emotionally charged moments in recent history, from the deadly sniper attacks in suburban Washington to the anguish of families grieving for loved ones killed in Iraq.

"In an inquiry focused on correcting the record and explaining how such fraud could have been sustained within the ranks of *The Times*, the *Times* journalists have so far uncovered new problems in at least 36 of the 73 articles

Mr. Blair wrote since he started getting national reporting assignments late last October. In the final months the audacity of the deceptions grew by the week, suggesting the work of a troubled young man veering toward professional self-destruction."

The *Times*, in the minds of many, was the most respected and credible newspaper in America. Blair, and a couple others, however, knocked it down a few notches.

Blair's unprofessional antics may have been the most serious—or at least talked about—since Janet Cooke of the *Washington Post* gave the world "Jimmy's World" in 1980. Cooke told the story of Jimmy, an "eight-year-old and a third-generation heroin addict, a precocious little boy with sandy hair, velvety brown eyes and needle marks freckling the baby-smooth skin of his thin brown arms."

Jimmy, she wrote, wanted to grow up to become a heroin dealer.

It was a compelling and sad story of a young boy caught in a hopeless world of violence and drugs.

Her work won a Pulitzer Prize in 1981.

There was a problem. Cooke, amid controversy, admitted there was no Jimmy and she had made up much of what she wrote.

There have been many other egregious examples between Cooke and Blair. Here is a brief rundown of some of the most visible and interesting issues of reporters and editors suffering "ethical lapses" that have contributed greatly to a loss in general media credibility.

Patricia Smith, a *Boston Globe* columnist, resigned in 1998 after fabricating people and quotes in her columns.

She said in her last column: "From time to time in my metro column, to create the desired impact or slam home a salient point, I attributed quotes to people who didn't exist. I could give them names, even occupations, but I couldn't give them what they needed most—a heartbeat. As anyone who's ever touched a newspaper knows, that's one of the cardinal sins of journalism: Thou shall not fabricate. No exceptions. No excuses."

Mike Barnicle, also a *Boston Globe* columnist who called for the resignation of Smith, resigned in 1998, while serving a suspension on accusations he made up sources and facts, and used and altered material from others— including comedian George Carlin.

Michael Vigh and Kevin Cantera, two reporters for the *Salt Lake Tribune*, were fired, and Editor Jay Shelledy re-signed in 2003, after the reporters took $10,000 each from the *National Enquirer* for information about the Elizabeth Smart abduction case. The American Press Institute's web page wrote the case "involves lies, money, threatened law-suits, newsroom treachery...and lessons learned the hard way."

The North County (Calif.) Times (near San Diego) apologized in 2003 for altering a photograph because the words "*San Diego Union-Tribune*"—a softball team spon-sor and the *Times*' chief competitor—were visible on the player's uniform.

A *San Francisco Chronicle* reporter, suspended after his arrest at a rally opposing the U.S. invasion of Iraq, lost his job a few days later. Henry Norr was among more than 1,300 people arrested for blocking public streets the morning after the Iraq war started. The *Chronicle* had previously distributed a memo alerting its staff to be "cautious and gain approval" from superiors before being involved in such activity. Norr claimed a sick day to attend the antiwar protest.

A reporter, for a television station in Minneapolis, opened a parked car's door and took a videotape in April of 2000 at a home where thirteen pit bull dogs had been seized and the homeowner had been charged with staging dogfights. The videotape was in plain view in the back seat of the car. The reporter said what he did was "aggressive reporting." The TV station's assistant news director said reporters "often move in gray areas."

The *Utica (N.Y.) Observer-Dispatch* fired associate editor Russ Davis in mid-May 2000 after he admitted to making up letters to the editor. "I wanted to make it seem that my columns provoked reader interest," Davis told the newspaper. The newspaper's publisher said, "He tampered with our single most important commodity: our credibility."

A *Boston Herald* reporter was caught in 2003 trying to bring into the United States a large painting and other Iraqi war souvenirs. The reporter defended his actions by saying, "These items were being routinely discarded and destroyed and clearly were of no value to the Iraqi people." And, a satellite truck engineer for Fox News Channel tried to smuggle a dozen Iraqi paintings into the country.

The editor of the *King County Journal* in the state of Washington agreed with law enforcement requests in 2003 to run a fake story about a staged arson in an effort to help authorities prove a convicted murderer was trying to reach out from his prison cell and hire someone to set fire to his mother-in-law's home. The editor said, "We have a responsibility to the community."

The *Los Angeles Times* fired one of its photographers in 2003 for altering a front-page photo of a British soldier and a group of Iraqi civilians. The photographer said he used a computer to combine elements of two photos to improve the composition.

Credibility—or a loss of it—has contributed the most, many believe, to the problems facing newspapers today, such as declines in circulation and readership.

In a recent research study, at Washington State University, of Generation Y—those between the ages of seven and twenty-five—one of the questions asked was: "What would it take for you to reconnect or rely upon a newspaper for news and information?" The number one response was "credibility."

Students surveyed said things like: "Make it more credible/truthful/factual"…"less biased"…"broader coverage"…"less liberal"…"various points of view/voices" and "trustworthy content."

It isn't surprising that credibility is an issue. The American Society of Newspaper Editors' web site lists more than thirty links to research projects or articles that were written about credibility over the past twenty-five years.

Some of the titles or topics included: "The Media and Their Credibility Under Scrutiny"…"Can the Press be Trusted?"…"All the News That's Fit to Correct"…"Let's Admit We Are Fallible"…"Differing Opinions: New

APME Study on Newspaper Credibility Reveals Some Wide Differences on How Journalism and the Public Perceive Newspapers"…"Does the Public Really Hate the Press?"…"Dimensions of Media Credibility: Highlights of the 1985 ASNE Survey"…"Defining and Measuring Credibility of Newspapers"…and "Credibility Must Take a Permanent Place in Newsroom Priorities."

Credibility might be the most important factor for consumers, but corporate profit margin and bottom-line mandates often trump the cost of accuracy and credibility.

In study after study, credibility is paramount. A few years ago, the president of ASNE was talking about a recent survey when he said,

> *"To regain public trust, newspapers need to do a better job editing out misspellings and misquotes, curb the use of unnamed sources and resist the temptation to sensationalize. Editors and publishers also need to tighten their reins on news copy and reestablish ties with readers outside the newsroom."*

ASNE's Journalism Credibility Project spent three years researching and experimenting (and spent $1.2 million) and came up with some simple messages—arguably not much different than what has been said for years. The suggestions included getting the basics right, confessing mistakes, and not only being accessible to readers but also involving them.

Newspapers that participated in the project worked on

problem areas such as accuracy, bias, sensationalism, and showing respect for readers by explaining and discussing decision-making processes.

Janet Weaver, executive editor of the Sarasota (Fla.) Herald Tribune, participated in the project. In an earlier report she had talked about the difficulty of being too defensive, pointing out the importance of learning how to listen to readers without arguing with them. She said, "We recognized that credibility isn't about the big stories, but about the details—which are very important to our readers."

But not too much later, her managing editor, Rosemary Armao, resigned after an E-mail argument (of sorts) with a reader who questioned political coverage. "I have to accept that I did something that could have hurt the paper, and I'm trying to set that right, at great personal cost," Armao said.

Weaver said, "It compromised our impartiality and cast questions on our ability to cover that race. As journalists, I don't believe we reveal our personal views...Rather than have any shadow over the paper, she thought it would be in the best interests of the paper to resign."

ASNE released some interesting statistics from its newspaper credibility study:

Thirty-five percent of 3,000 U.S. adults surveyed by telephone say they see spelling or grammatical mistakes in their newspapers more than once a week.

Twenty-three percent say they find factual errors in the news stories of their daily papers at least once a week.

Seventy-three percent have become more skeptical about news accuracy.

Seventy-eight percent agree there is bias in the news

media.

Fifty-eight percent believe the public's dissatisfaction with the media is justified.

Fifty percent believe there are particular people or groups who get a "special break" in news coverage.

Seventy-eight percent believe powerful people or organizations can influence a newspaper to kill or "spin" a story.

Eighty-six percent believe the names of suspects should not be published until formal charges are filed.

Clearly, credibility is a two-way street for journalists and readers/letter writers.

Chapter Sixteen

With Warmest Regards

"Don't Hit A Man When He's Down—Kick Him, It's Easier." That was the message a high school junior once printed on business-sized cards in his print shop class.

As a senior, his printing expertise stepped up a notch when one class project was to print the family name on napkins that Mom could use on special occasions. It was a good project, except for one unfortunate soul who purchased and brought to school sanitary napkins, rather than dinner napkins.

The reporter-editor referenced many times in stories in this book, was once a high school kid, much like the sons and daughters we've all known. At seventeen, he really didn't know where he was going in life. He did, however, know a thing or two about printing.

He wasn't exceptionally smart, or at least his overall high school grade point average was a shade under 3.0. But he was organized. OK, maybe the right word is anal. Whatever, he had taken most of his required courses before his senior year, which allowed him to take electives—two school periods every day—of print shop.

It was quite the deal. He knew where to locate every letter in a California job case. He knew how to set type in a stick. He knew how to lock the type in a form, using a key and little square blocks. He knew how to put the form on a letterpress, ink the plate, and make impressions. Shoot, he could even operate an offset camera and press.

That turned out to be his ticket to a college education and career as a newspaperman.

When it came time to enroll in college he was offered a full-ride scholarship to L.A. Trade Tech, but his parents persuaded him to see if he could get a scholarship to Pepperdine University. His father was a Church of Christ minister and Pepperdine was affiliated with the Church of Christ.

To his surprise, he was also offered a full-ride scholarship to attend Pepperdine. He would operate an offset camera and offset press the university was soon to purchase, to save significant printing costs.

He was told to major in journalism. Back in those days, he did what he was told.

For four years the university did not purchase the printing equipment he was gifted to operate, so he continued to take journalism courses and graduated with a bachelor's degree.

Was it a twist of fate, or God's hand?

He was lucky to take those print shop classes, even

though his parents complained often that he was wasting his time.

It's funny what the brain retains. To this day he wonders about his print-shop buddy, Mike, who sniffed a solvent rag for two hours a day. He wonders what happened to poor Mike, his high school's king of the stoners.

He always knew solvent was good, but only to clean ink off hands and mechanical devices.

Without his printing background, he likely never would have worked in the newspaper industry, and been subjected to readers who often had little positive to say.

Here are some final miscellaneous shots in an attempt to "Kill the Editor."

JOURNALISTIC EXPERTS:

Is the customer always right? Not when it comes to readers. Yet many letter writers, regardless of their background, believe they are experts in writing, journalism, and the newspaper business. It often isn't enough to publish in print the ground rules for letter writers, including the fact that newspapers reserve the right to edit letters for clarity, libel, and space requirements. If you change one word—or even correct punctuation—you have seriously wronged the writer and have no morals or integrity. The following letter writer had a minor change made to her copy before her letter was published. That minor elimination did not change the substance of the letter, but did protect the newspaper from a potential charge of libel.

A letter appeared in your newspaper over my name. That letter was not, however, the letter which I had written to the editor three weeks earlier. In my naiveté, I was unaware letters to the editor are edited prior to printing.

I wrote to make a particular point in response to an earlier letter. That point, however, was removed—along with the portions of my letter which your editor saw fit to remove. What remained said nothing, merely took up space, and was an embarrassment to me. Had I been consulted, as journalistic integrity would seem to me to dictate, I would have requested the letter remain unprinted, rather than edited.

Please cancel my subscription to the newspaper immediately. If you cannot accurately reprint a typed letter, I have no confidence you can accurately report the news.

A SUCKER IS BORN EVERY MINUTE:
Scams have been around virtually since the beginning of time. Chain letters and pyramids are common. But one innovative international scam—still alive today—surfaced when the following letter arrived from Lagos, Nigeria:

It is trust and confidence that I write to make this urgent and important business proposal to you. I am the chief accountant with the Nigerian National Petroleum Corporation (NNPC) here in Lagos, Nigeria.

I have been assigned by my colleague to seek a foreign partner in the transfer of the sum of U.S. $25.5 million.

This money arose from deliberate over-invoicing of a particular contract awarded by the ministry in 1993. We have been safe-guarding this money since then, awaiting an appropriate time when the money can be transferred into a safe account.

Now, the presidency has ordered that all debts owed to the foreign contractors by the government should be paid immediately in order not to over burden the federal government with the debt. On the strength of this order, we wish to take advantage of it to present your company as the bonafide [sic] beneficiary of the money.

To carry out this transaction successfully, we would require your banking particulars, account number, name of beneficiary, telephone, FAX and telex number of your bank. And if need arises, I will invite you to Lagos, Nigeria to see things yourself.

We have agreed to share the money with you as follows:

60% will be for all parties in Nigeria.

30% will be for your providing the necessary assistance.

The remaining 10% have been mapped out for incidental expenses that might be incurred throughout the transaction by both parties.

The nature of your company's business is irrelevant to this transaction as all arrangements have been concluded for a successful hitch-free transaction.

We have also taken measure to ensure there are no risks involved on your part at all. Reach me on the above at 234-1-1522083. We have estimated this transaction will be concluded within 14 working days on receipt of your bank information. Also FAX to me your private telephone and

FAX numbers for easy communication.
   This business is strictly confidential and urgent.
   Best regards,

THE MORE THINGS CHANGE, THE MORE THEY STAY THE SAME:
The following E-mail arrived in late September 2003.

Dear Friend,

Good day, sorry to surprise you and take some of your time in going through this unexpected letter of plea for your understanding and assistance.

This message may come as a surprise as we have not met, but we are desperately in need of help. I got this contact out of desperation and frustration, via a comprehensive search on the Internet.

I cannot contact any of my late father's associates because of the precarious situation in my country and the predicament facing my family.

I am the son of the erst-while leader of the Movement for the Total Independence of Angola (UNITA), Jonas Savimbi, who was killed in a fierce gun battle with government troops loyal to Eduardo Dos Santos on the 22nd of February 2002.

My name is Saikita Savimbi, son of Jonas Savimbi. I was aware of sales of diamonds and crude oil to individuals and countries that clandestinely came to purchase these products.

After the PEACE ACCORD was broken, the United States of America government abandoned my father and the United Nations (UN) imposed sanctions on all products coming out of UNITA controlled areas. It is from the proceeds of these sales that were used by UNITA to purchase arms to prosecute their war agenda.

My late father, Jonas Savimbi, deposited large sums of funds in Europe realized from the sale of diamonds with a Security company that he intended to make further purchases with over there.

My mother Catarina Savimbi is in possesion of the documents and informations of the deposit and all that it would take to be released to you on our behalf.

Our movements presently (including me) are highly restricted. We are forbidden to either travel abroad or out of our localities.

At the moment, US $28.5 Million Dollars cash my father transferred to and deposited in Europe before his death for these purchases he intended to make is safe and still with the Security firm.

We have the pass-code (P.I.N) and the documents for the deposited funds in the Security firm.

This is where your help is being sought, because presently we cannot travel to effect the release ourselves. We want to act fast before the government finds out about these funds or they will be confiscated as they did with several others. With this Personal Identification Number (PIN) pass-code and other information and power of attorney you will be able to proceed to the Security firm on behalf of my family for the collection on our behalf.

When you inform us of your readiness, I will give you all the information needed before you can get access to the funds you will then proceed to the Security company where the consignment of funds will be released to you.

We shall negotiate favorably with you what you will be entitled to as you will be instructed to also set up fresh accounts for the family with names and information that shall be relayed to you as we progress.

Please get back to me with your intentions to help to enable me to give you the full details and information to collecting the money on our behalf. We need the money to be able to finance all family members into Europe where we are assured of political asylum status by the European Economic Community.

DUE TO THESE CIRCUMSTANCES YOUR CONFIDENTIALITY IN THIS TRANSACTION IS REQUIRED TO PREVENT MY GOVERNMENT FROM KNOWING ABOUT OUR PLANS AND FUTURE INTENTIONS OF ELOPING INTO EUROPE.

Thanks once again for your time.

Sincerely Yours,

Saikita Savimbi

IT WAS ONLY A TWO-LETTER WORD:

It was only a two-letter word, but the result was a more than 500-word letter to the editor after "it" was used incorrectly in an editorial. It proved, yet once again, the old adage that some people have far too much free time. The following letter has more than anyone would ever want to know about the dictionary. It is an incredible example of absurdity.

The word "it" should not be the first word of the first sentence of the first paragraph of any utterance, written or spoken unless the word "it" is the subject being discussed.

It: pronoun, the nominative and objective singular neuter pronoun of the third person, used: 1. As a substitute for a specific noun or name when referring to things or places, or when referring to infants or animals or unspecified sex. 2. To represent some implied idea, condition, action or situation: How far was it? I'm opposed to it. 3. As the subject or predicate nominative of a verb whose logical subject is anticipated: Who is it? It is John.

Some dictionaries do continue on to give examples of "it." 4. As the indefinite subject of a verb introducing a clause or a phrase: It seems that he knew. 5. As the indefinite object after certain verbs in idiomatic expressions: to brazen it out.

In certain children's games, the player required to perform some specific act.

The making of a dictionary is both a science and an art. The painstaking accumulation of reliable data, consisting of thousands upon thousands of individual facts of the language;

The proper classification of this data; and finally the formulation of sound conclusions from this mass of material—all illustrate the inductive process about the language, the phrasing of definitions, and the ordering of word treatments demand of the lexicographer the ability to manipulate the language with economy and precision. The science without the art is likely to be ineffective; the art without the science is certain to be inaccurate.

The dictionary is not a tool to be used hastily or casually. Status or usage labels may throw light upon the way in which a total context should be interpreted or upon the style of a writer. The etymology, though by no means an arbiter of current use, can be revealing about past use and suggestive as to the connotations of present use.

In short, the dictionary has a wealth of information about the language to offer, but, like any other form of wealth, it calls for wise and judicious use.

Let him view his dictionary not as a series of ex cathedra pronouncements, nor as holy writ, but a reference word, a body of data about the language, deriving its authority from the care and completeness with which the facts were collected and interpreted.

The use, spelling, and pronunciation of any word are correct only when they are commonly and unaffectedly used by cultivated and educated people in a manner that does not call unfavorable attention to the user/s.

A dictionary is not an authority to determine and state what is correct, but a reflection of what is in use among cultivated and educated people.

Since there are variations, even among these cultivated and educated people in the various parts of the country, there are too many variations for any one book to record all of those currently in proper usage. The mere fact that any one word, its spelling, pronunciation, or usage is left out does not, in and of itself, prove it cannot be accepted as proper. However, it can be a guide in determining what is proper.

We do not have any body comparable to the United States Bureau of Standards that can state with authority that a purported inch, foot, mile, etc., does not measure correctly. Words, their usage, spelling, etc., cannot be dictated so precisely, but the use can only be compared to what cultivated, educated people in the various parts of the Country are in the habit of using. What may once have been totally and ridiculously improper at one time may at another time be accepted as proper.

Although the word "it" is in the process of being accepted as you used it in your Editorial, total acceptance is yet to be.

A NOT-SO-HAPPY SOUL:

The following was included in a column discussing a new redesign of the newspaper. "I trust that you approve of the new, eye-catching look of our favorite newspaper. If you're not quite used to it yet, give it time. If an old traditionalist like me can embrace such a dramatic change, it'll win you over as well." The reader's response:

No way! It's a "family" paper—which members outnumber single-person households. You pull ALL of Mom's articles back-to-back with kids' comics—Dad's big puzzle,

Jumble, Cryptoquotes, Celebrity Cipher on the comic sheet—kids are not going to do these! And Dad isn't going to wait until kids get finished with comics—and Mom shouldn't either. Kids don't read Heloise, Ann Landers, Dr. Gott, Bombeck—you can't cut up the comics to pass parts around to all. Only a single-person home can be "won over." He gets to have the paper all to himself (herself).

AND FINALLY, SOME BRIEF PARTING SHOTS:

Your paper is the caliber of "Tonya Harding"—no class, "zilch." You made sure you wrote a column on her false accusations of burglary, but nothing on Nancy Kerrigan's wedding! I'm glad I'm not a subscriber to your delinquent paper. Wake up you stupid idiots and report classy news—not trash!

Your new TV section format stinks to high heaven...I hope whoever designed it and approved it gets lockjaw and seasickness at the same time.

You are a mediocre paper constantly becoming medio-cre(er)...Management needs its collective bottom kicked for this decision.

With Warmest Regards

You have taken a wonderful small-town mainly retirement community newspaper and converted it to a Big Town, or City, paper that I and most of the citizens have very little use for unless one happens to be a source of old unwanted papers for bulk resale or for recycling purposes.

In an emergency, your newspaper is a poor substitute to use to wipe my bottom with. I dare you to print this in your now stupid paper.

Index

Acknowledgments

A book like this could never have been written without letter writers. Without those words, and the time spent crafting them, these pages wouldn't be nearly as shocking or readable.

Thanks.

There are many others who need to be acknowledged, for a variety of reasons.

It's common when a television announcer is interviewing an athlete who was instrumental in a victory for the star to begin by thanking his "Lord and Savior Jesus Christ."

I, too, acknowledge Him. He has been good to me, and has watched over me through my life, including some times I'd like to forget.

I also thank my wife, Lisa, who has always been there, even if only at times in my mind, and I have lived happily with her over the past several years. She wasn't physically with me for many of my experiences as an editor, but she has been with me for the highest of highs and some of the lowest of lows.

Our marriage is good, and she helps me keep not only my sanity, but perspective.

I also want to thank Derren, Dustin, Noah, and Hank Aaron Irby—my four sons. In many ways they have transformed my life, and they are the subjects of my current writing project: *Life With Kids*. While their stories in the next book won't be as bizarre as most of the stories in *Kill the Editor*, they are certainly funnier and more upbeat—the kids and the stories.

Alex Tan is the director of the Edward R. Murrow School of Communication at Washington State University. He's my boss. I owe him a great debt of gratitude for his support and good judgment in accepting the recommendation for my hire as a professor of journalism. He's also, hands down, the best boss I've ever had.

I also appreciate the collegiality of those who serve on the faculty in Washington State's School of Communication. I'm blessed in my second career with wonderful, supportive colleagues.

In my newspaper career, I need to first acknowledge Bob Bentley, another very good boss and mentor who taught me a lot about writing, editing, friendship, and leadership. He was a pretty fair basketball player, but I was better.

I also want to thank the other bosses I had in my newspaper life, some of whom weren't as supportive, including John, Tony, and Steve. I learned how not to do certain things from each of you.

Pete and Paul, thanks for your confidence in me; but I

think you became too reactionary when you became corporate managers.

Joe, you were fun.

Carl, you were great, and our parting was my fault.

I must also acknowledge my many stops in the newspaper industry. We are vagabonds and we learn much along the way as we seek promotions, and new and exciting assignments. Thanks for the education and recreation at the *Alhambra (Calif.) Post-Advocate, Glendale and Burbank (Calif.) Daily Review, Pacific Palisades (Calif.) Palisadian*; *Nevada State Journal* and *Reno Evening Gazette*; *Great Falls (Mont.) Tribune*; *San Francisco Chronicle, Thousand Oaks (Calif.) News Chronicle, Bakersfield Californian, Tulare (Calif.) Advance-Register, Ventura (Calif.) Star, San Gabriel (Calif.) Valley Tribune*; *Anderson (Ind.) Herald-Bulletin*; and *Shawano (Wis.) Leader*.

Some other reporters, editors, and newspaper managers and journalists who deserve recognition for helping to make me who I am today include C. T. Nelson, my college journalism adviser; Charlie Hushaw, Copley Editorial Training Program mentor; Warner Jenkins, *Alhambra-Post Advocate* editor; Mike Trihey, the best reporter I have ever known; and my sports buddies—Steve Sneddon, Mike Blackwell, Ray Hagar, Joe Howry, Mike Griffith, Jeff Evans, Jim Hodges, Rob Walters; and many others.

Lifelong friends, sometimes close and sometimes not so close, are hard to come by. I'm sure I've had a few, but one comes to mind. Thanks Squirrel.

I wouldn't be here without Bob and Pauline Irby, so thanks Dad and Mom. And I wouldn't be as thick-skinned if I hadn't had two older sisters; thanks Reba Witwer and Susan Easterling. My apologies to Reba's husband, Bob Witwer, for repeatedly whipping him when he started dating my sister.

Clearly, I love and appreciate all of my family members, including my mother-in-law, Violet Therrien, and her dog companion, Toby.

Finally, I'd like to acknowledge American Book Publishing and my editor, Leticia Gómez. Leticia was a pleasure to work with and I think she enjoyed my brief updates as much as I did her E-mails.

Thanks to all.

About the Author

John is an associate professor in the Edward R. Murrow School of Communication at Washington State University in Pullman, Washington. He teaches news writing and reporting, news editing, public affairs reporting, sports reporting, public relations techniques and media usage, and media ethics.

He joined the WSU journalism faculty in the fall of 1999 after more than twenty-five years experience in newspapers. John began his career in community journalism as a reporter and photographer at a 4,000-circulation weekly in Southern California, and later worked as an editor at the 450,000-circulation San Francisco Chronicle. He has also held the publisher's job at small and medium-sized daily newspapers, and was editor-in-chief of two newspaper groups with more than 100,000 circulation.

John and his wife, Lisa, have four sons, Derren, eighteen: Dustin, fourteen; Noah, eight; and Hank Aaron Irby, five. Personal interests include writing, family, religion, the Internet, reading, films, art, music, sports, and travel.